Regards,
from
Chris

THE BEST TWELVE YEARS

PETER GOULD

Warren Maginn
Designer & Editor

© Copyright 2005 Peter Gould.
All rights reserved. No part of this publication may be reproduced, stored in a retrieval system, or transmitted, in any form or by any means, electronic, mechanical, photocopying, recording, or otherwise, without the written prior permission of the author.

Note for Librarians: A cataloguing record for this book is available from Library and Archives Canada at www.collectionscanada.ca/amicus/index-e.html
ISBN 1-4120-5523-7

Printed in Victoria, BC, Canada. Printed on paper with minimum 30% recycled fibre. Trafford's print shop runs on "green energy" from solar, wind and other environmentally-friendly power sources.

TRAFFORD
PUBLISHING™

Offices in Canada, USA, Ireland and UK
This book was published *on-demand* in cooperation with Trafford Publishing. On-demand publishing is a unique process and service of making a book available for retail sale to the public taking advantage of on-demand manufacturing and Internet marketing. On-demand publishing includes promotions, retail sales, manufacturing, order fulfilment, accounting and collecting royalties on behalf of the author.

Book sales for North America and international:
Trafford Publishing, 6E–2333 Government St.,
Victoria, BC v8t 4p4 CANADA
phone 250 383 6864 (toll-free 1 888 232 4444)
fax 250 383 6804; email to orders@trafford.com
Book sales in Europe:
Trafford Publishing (uk) Limited, 9 Park End Street, 2nd Floor
Oxford, UK OXI IHH United Kingdom
phone 44 (0)1865 722 113 (local rate 0845 230 9601)
facsimile 44 (0)1865 722 868; info.uk@trafford.com
Order online at:
trafford.com/05-0421

10 9 8 7 6 5 4 3 2

To my grandson Warren,
without whose intense interest and perpetual persistence,
this book would not have been written.

CHAPTER CONTENTS

CHAPTER 1	IN THE BEGINNING	9
CHAPTER 2	A PASSAGE FROM INDIA	13
CHAPTER 3	HALTON	25
CHAPTER 4	GROUND STAFF	45
CHAPTER 5	LEARNING TO FLY	61
CHAPTER 6	LANCASTERS	75
CHAPTER 7	WAR AND PEACE	121
CHAPTER 8	INDIA REVISITED	135
CHAPTER 9	BRIZE NORTON	161
CHAPTER 10	THE BERLIN AIR LIFT	189
CHAPTER 11	RELOCATION	201
CHAPTER 12	REFLECTIONS	221
APPENDIX	THE IMMORTAL TEN THOUSAND	

1
IN THE BEGINNING

"Cor!" I exclaimed with a sharp intake of breath, "Twelve years!" I was sitting with others around a large table in the school library. I was fifteen years old and twelve years seemed to be about the rest of my life. I was studying a coloured brochure sent by the RAF, featuring life as an Apprentice at Halton (The premier technical training base of the RAF). "What's that?" asked Mr. Serdival, the English master, from across the table. I passed the brochure to him which he studied for a short time, then sliding it back said, "And they'll be the best twelve years of your life."

I came from a military family and before World War II, half the British Army was permanently based in India. My father had completed his Army time and had opted to take his discharge in India where he then held a well-paid job on the railway. He was based at the large new maintenance facility half way between Bombay and Delhi, that had been carved out of the bush. Although it had a number of facilities, educationally it was restricted to one primary school, consequentially his four children were in boarding school in Bombay.

For him the down side of life in India was that everything had to be paid for, and the school fees accounted for much of his salary. Indian independence was on the horizon and most of the British were making plans to return to the UK. He and his family would have their passages paid by the railway on his retirement. His problem was, that by then, I would be too old to be counted as a dependant. Those were not the days of cheap travel and so he had to find a way of getting me to England at minimum cost.

He had sent for a leaflet, which he showed me, featuring life as an Army Apprentice at the training school at Chepstow. To get there, a free passage could be obtained on a troopship. The idea did not in the least appeal to me and as I had always been mad on flying, I countered by sending for the RAF version which also included the troopship. My father was delighted and immediately put arrangements in hand, for me to take the entrance exam.

The entrance exam was a competitive one but restricted to English, Maths and Science, fortunately my best subjects. Nevertheless I was given my own private curriculum to the exclusion of all other subjects. Eventually the day of the exam dawned. My whole future seemed to depend on it. I was given lots of good wishes and some well-intentioned advice, like emptying my bowels, which seemed unnecessary as the stress of the exam threatened to do that. The long days of waiting for the result seemed endless. September 3rd 1939, and the start of World War II came and went, but little changed. One day, eventually, my parents were informed that I had been accepted and that was the day my school days ended. I went home for a prolonged Christmas holiday and to prepare for the great adventure.

2
A PASSAGE FROM INDIA

It was 18th. February 1940, the embarkation date advised by the authorities. The whole family were assembled on the key-side at Bombay docks. Moored alongside was HMT Lancashire, a ship of 16,000 tons. A troop ship, grey in colour and somewhat old fashioned in appearance. Not in the least like the luxury liners that used to anchor in Bombay harbour and extend invitations to come on board and inspect their opulence.

Life in India for the ex-patriot British, was very UK orientated and we were always keenly aware that we lived in a foreign country. Like me, most of my contemporaries had been born in India and never been out of it. I often used to gaze out over the vast expanse of ocean to the west and think "Somewhere out there is England." Now I was about to realise every British child's dream, to go to England. Yet the excitement gradually gave way to apprehension as I stepped aboard. My first thoughts when I viewed the scene below decks was that it reminded me of the old eighteenth century slave ships. The 'mess deck,' as it was called, which served as living quarters as well, was open plan and extended from front to rear of the ship without a watertight bulkhead. The roof of the deck had rows and rows of stout steel rings fixed to it and to these, we learned in due course, hammocks were slung, everybody's standard bedding. The headroom throughout the deck was about seven ft.

Eventually came the sailing hour. The family were very British and stiff upper lip as they said their farewells not knowing when or if we would ever see each other again.

On deck the ship's rail was relatively empty as I stood waving goodbye. Almost all the passengers were young soldiers going home to join the B.E.F. (British Expeditionary Force) in France. They had no one at whom to wave. I stayed a long time on deck watching the ship plough its way out of the harbour, then swing to starboard and the west across that vast ocean at which I had stared so longingly.

Returning to the mess deck I learned that I was one of eighteen boys all heading for RAF Halton. Sixteen of them were from two Army schools, one in the Himalayas and one in the Nilgary Hills in south India. Their fathers were still in the Army. They tended to band together in two groups to the exclusion of Doug Sofa and me who were both from two different schools in Bombay. All eighteen of us boys were in the charge of two Sergeants who had served in India for twelve years. When it was time for our first meal, two long tables were lowered from the deck roof, where they were held suspended, along with forms on either side, and these accommodated all twenty of us, eighteen boys and the two Sergeants.

By common consent, it was too hot in the tropics to sleep in the mess deck so everyone took their bedding up on deck to sleep under the stars. We formed a long row of sleeping figures stretching from stem to stern and slept peacefully 'till morning.

The deck had a gentle slope from front to rear and alongside the deck rail ran a four-inch water pipe with an open-ended gate valve at the high point at the front of the ship. At first light the still quiet of the night, accompanied by the monotonous muffled roar of the bow wash, was suddenly shattered by the loud cry of "Swabbers!!" What seemed like a flash flood of water bore relentlessly down the deck. In a thrice the line of sleepers were on their feet gathering up their bedding and stepping back to let the tidal wave flow by. This was the daily ritual for the eight mornings that the ship was in tropical waters.

By now I was beginning to suffer from severe 'home sickness'. I found myself alone in a hostile environment. I knew nobody and nobody seemed to want to know me, except Doug Sofa to whom I seemed to gravitate, though we had little in common. The military schoolboys resented any intrusion into their little circles and overtures of friendship from any of the troops invariably proved to have sexual connotations. I have never, before or since, felt so desperately lonely and dejected.

On the fifth day we arrived at Aden on the mouth of the Red Sea, a sleepy little port squeezed between the desert and the sea. We anchored in the harbour, took on a few supplies and sailed again after a few hours. Once again it was the same ritual always accompanied by the muffled roar of the bow wash. At night I would stare at the passing sea, glowing with phosphorescence.

One day all the boys were busy writing letters home, which would be posted in a day or two in Port Suez, our next port of call. A vociferous young ginger haired soldier wandered up to our corner, surveyed us and said, "Writing home to Mother, are we?" Then turned to his companion and said, "I haven't written to my fuckin' mother for seven fuckin' years, when I get home the fucker'll die." More than a little shocked and disgusted, we all pretended not to have heard and busied ourselves in our writing while our visitors wandered aimlessly away.

On the third day out of Aden we arrived at Port Suez at the entrance to the Suez Canal. Once again we anchored in the harbour, this time all night, then entered the canal in the morning. The canal stretches for 100 miles and connects with two lakes known as 'the Great Bitter Lake' and 'the Little Bitter Lake.' It was the strangest experience standing on the deck and watching the land glide by. Through the lakes it was full speed ahead and by nightfall we had reached Port Said, at the other end of the canal.

The next morning the ship was a hive of activity. We anchored in the harbour, while supply boats were plying backwards and forwards to the shore and pressing against the hull all round the ship, were some twenty or so "Bum Boats." These were small craft laden with goodies for sale. A roaring trade was being done between the soldiers and the Egyptian boatmen. As dusk fell we weighed anchor and headed out into the Mediterranean.

Now that we had left the tropics behind we were in the European theatre and had our first indication that we were heading into war. We were no longer alone on the sea. With us and in front of us at all times, was a Royal Navy destroyer. Both ships continuously zig zagged to deter a U-boat attack. As the land faded astern a sudden burst of cheering arose from the deck full of soldiers, their khaki drill uniforms replaced by surge. They threw their 'Solar Topee' helmets high into the air and over the side of the ship. For two hundred years or more it was firmly believed that the tropical sun on a bear head would cause 'sun stroke,' though nobody seemed able to describe exactly what sun stroke was or why the native Indians seemed unaffected. At some time during World War II the solar topee, which had been worn universally by soldiers and civilians alike, ceased to exist.

Now the sleeping arrangements also changed. The top deck was abandoned in favour of the mess deck, where hammocks were slung every night, suspended from the heavy metal rings, fixed to the deck roof. Life was now lived below decks, both on the mess deck and the decks below. These contained the galley, toilets etc. The top deck was used only for stretching ones legs and taking the air.

Deep in the bowels of the ship was a little area where, every night, some mysterious activity would take place. On going down to explore, I discovered that it was a gambling game called "Crown and Anchor." It was controlled by a rather resourceful and extravert soldier and consisted of a printed linen sheet approximately 3 ft. x 18 in., divided into six equal segments in two rows of three. Each of the corner segments displayed a red heart, a red diamond, a black club or a black spade. The two centre segments displayed pictures, one of a crown and the other an anchor. Two dice, bearing the same six icons, were being continuously rolled to shouts of, "Three to one the old jam tart, two to one the spade, or five to one the old mud hook, four to one the crown." Money was flowing backwards and forwards across the board, most of it towards the controller. As gambling was strictly forbidden on military premises, lookouts were posted at all approaches to the area and at the first hint of danger, the linen board along with the stake money, would disappear in an instant.

One day I was standing in a queue to use the toilets. These consisted of a room approximately 35 ft. x 20 ft. with three cubicles set against the long wall opposite the entrance and alongside them, an open area with a trough containing running sea water that continued under the seats in the cubicles. The doors to all three cubicles were closed and the queue extended beyond the entrance to the toilets. Suddenly a large, exuberant soldier, carrying some newspaper for use as toilet paper, barged his way into the toilet area and eyeing the closed doors, said in a loud voice "Full up is it? I'll soon move the buggers." Wherewith, he rustled up the paper into a large bunch and set fire to it, then dropped it into the open trough. The burning paper, floating on the flowing water, was carried into the cubicles from whence came three startled cries, then three doors flung open, and three unfortunates emerged with their trousers around their ankles.

After four days of zig zagging our way through the Mediterranean, the grey coast of France loomed into sight and specifically, the port of Marseilles. Here the ship berthed alongside a dock, and having been secured by mooring ropes, no further action seemed to be intended that day.

The next morning we were told that all the troops, for recreation, were to go on a route march around the city and that, if we wished, we boys could tag along at the back of them. The idea of walking again on Terra Firma was appealing and all eighteen of us joined the column. The weather was cloudy but dry and a fresh March wind was blowing. The route march lasted about two hours when, as we were approaching the return to the ship, a particle of foreign matter found its way into my eye. As soon as we went on board I made straight for the ablutions where I took off my jacket and proceeded to try and wash the offending particle from my eye. Still rubbing it, I made my way back to the boy's mess area where a meal was being started. Half way through the meal a soldier came into our mess area holding a jacket. "This belong to anyone?" he asked. At once I realised that it was mine and that I had, rather carelessly, left it in the ablutions. The jacket was handed to me and I immediately felt in the inside pocket for the five pound note that my father had given me. It was meant to last until the RAF started paying me. Alas it was gone.

Although my financial requirements were modest, the thought of being penniless in this strange and hostile world had a numbing effect. While I sat contemplating my options, the rest of the boys seemed to have formed into a group in which there was much murmuring. Eventually one of them approached me holding out his open hand containing a number of coins. He said, "We've collected two pounds, seventeen and six pence, which might get you through." "Oh thanks very much," I said and thought, "Maybe they're not so hostile after all." However, they still maintained their defences against all strangers.

The next day was spent wandering aimlessly around the ship waiting for something to happen but apart from some shunting of railway rolling stock on the key-side, nothing much more happened. The next morning, however, it was all systems go. Disembarkation and entrainment was the order of the day. It was late afternoon before all the troops, along with us eighteen boys, were satisfactorily ensconced in the passenger compartments of a French train. The boys, along with our two Sergeant minders, were housed in three compartments. Two contained the boys of each of the two respective military schools while the third had been allocated to the two Sergeants, Doug Sofa, myself and two of the military school boys who seemed to have been rejected by their fellows. These two lads had one thing in common, they were both extremely thin, a useful feature when it came to bedtime. As dusk fell the train reluctantly pulled out of the sidings and onto the main line, then headed steadily into the gathering darkness. It seemed that everything on the railway had priority over us. Our stops were frequent and our progress slow.

At the appropriate hour we turned our minds to the sleeping arrangements for the night. We soon found that our two Sergeant minders had already worked this out and now intended to put their plan into action. The Sergeants would stretch out on the two seats. Doug Sofa and I would sleep, head to foot, on the floor between the seats and the two very thin lads would be hoisted up into the luggage racks at roof level above the seats where they remained immobile. Whenever they wished to turn over during the night, they would call out and Doug Sofa and I would get up and turn them over. Sometimes the Sergeants would condescend to take a turn. The heating system in the compartments of this train consisted of a metal grating about 30cm wide, let into the floor, and lying midway between the seats. This strip extended from the compartment window to the door leading into the corridor. At first Doug and I were quite pleased that our bed was on this heater as we would hardly need a blanket. However, the heating proved to be less than reliable. It came on very hot for a while and then switched off altogether. As a result we spent all night throwing off our blankets and then piling them on again.

So the journey proceeded slowly all through the next day when, as we headed north, we had our first sight of snow and put our hands out of the window to see what it felt like. Most of us had never seen snow in our lives and even the boys from the Himalayan School had only seen it as white peaks in the far distance. We chugged our way through another night like the first. The cold periods, when the heating was off, were getting colder and as the new day dawned we were relieved to see that we were approaching a city which proved to be Cherbourg. We were beginning to feel the cold now. Having lived all our lives in the tropics our bodies were not acclimatised. Although we were wearing suits of a kind, they were mostly made of fabric more suitable for a warm climate. I was wearing one of my uncle's cast off suits and the shirt was so much too big for me that, whenever I displeased our Sergeants, they would threaten to throw me through my collar.

The train pulled into the dock area and came to a final halt opposite a jetty. A cross-channel steamer was tethered alongside. At a leisurely pace we all began to evacuate the train and embark on the ship which eventually sailed for Southampton. Some five hours later the ship docked at Southampton and the troops began to disembark. This was when we said goodbye to our minders. We remained on board to await the arrival of their replacement from the RAF, who would escort us to Halton. Months later, when the events of Dunkirk began to unfold, we wondered how many of our shipmates had survived the breath-taking evacuation.

It soon became apparent that our new custodian would not be there that day and with the Army Sergeants gone, we were nominally in the charge of the ship's Captain. He had too many distractions to be overly concerned about our general welfare. So, having sorted ourselves out some suitable sleeping accommodation, we all went ashore to savour the delights of Southampton. This was our first city night spent in a country at war, and the dominating experience was the black out. The whole city was in total darkness. Us boys immediately split up into our standard divisions. The two groups of military schoolboys leaving Doug Sofa and myself to our own devices.

We wandered down a darkened street looking for some sign of life. We eventually came to a restaurant with its entrance door in very subdued lighting. It proved to be a fish restaurant with a bar type counter. Ranged along the counter were a number of bar stools. A few tables and chairs occupied the rest of the public area. We took our seats on the bar stools and prepared to enjoy our first taste of the famous British 'fish and chips.' Whilst waiting for the food to arrive, we discussed, questioningly, the protocol for tipping in English restaurants. Neither of us had any idea. When the food arrived and payment was required, Doug Sofa handed over the required sum. With some coins still in his hand he asked the waitress "And how much for you"? Without answering, the waitress left. A short time later, whilst in the middle of our meal, I heard a sound like a slap on the far side of Doug Sofa and on the bar along side him, was a piece of raw fish. It was obvious that the waitress had thrown this at him. Deeply embarrassed, we pretended it hadn't happened, finished our meal and hurriedly left.

The next morning the RAF representative came aboard. Gathering us together, he led us to the railway station to await the London train. The journey to London seemed a model of speed and efficiency compared with the tortuous trek across France and we were looking forward to our first sight of London. Alas the only part of London that we saw was Waterloo station and Baker Street station, the connective journey being by underground. However, we were thrilled to experience the 'London Tube.'

From Baker Street the train took about an hour to arrive at the picturesque little village of Wendover, about 5 miles short of Aylesbury. From here we were walked the mile or so to the barrack blocks of No.2 wing at RAF Halton, which was to be our new home. It was also the last time that we were walked anywhere. From then on, we were marched.

3
HALTON

Halton presented a somewhat grim picture in a beautiful setting. It consisted of four separate groups of barrack blocks known as wings. Each wing contained three barrack blocks arranged one in front of the other referred to as squadrons. Separating numbers one and two wings, and serving both, was a large parade ground. It was the same with numbers three and four wings. The whole compendium was tucked into a ridge of the Chiltern Hills that extended for some 10 miles. At the eastern end was Chequers, the country residence of the prime minister.

On arrival, the boys from India were distributed between the three squadrons of number two wing. The military school boys in A and B squadron while Doug Sofa and myself found ourselves, still together, in C squadron. The whole wing now consisted of some 600 boys who constituted the '41st Entry.'

Each of us was allocated a bed. This consisted of a steel framed structure laced with broad steel lattices. It was in two sections, that telescoped into each other. The mattress was in three equal squares called 'biscuits' and we were soon shown how the whole assortment had to be arranged every morning. The bed was to be closed up to half its sleeping length with the biscuits placed on it, one on top of the other. The two sheets were then to be sandwiched between two blankets, while a third blanket wrapped around the whole arrangement, all of which was then placed on top of the biscuits. Finally this whole configuration had to face towards the centre isle of the barrack room.

Next we were allocated 'room jobs'. The daily chores were divided between the twenty or so boys in each barrack room, while the common areas, such as the toilets and ablutions, were shared with the occupants of the room across the far side of the stairwell. These jobs had to be carried out daily, before breakfast spotless and shining, and were subjected to a daily inspection by Fred Barnes, the squadron Warrant Officer. Fred was a good leader and soon had us proud of our squadron identity. We even had a squadron song:

"We are Fred Barney's Army, the boys of shiny 'C'
We cannot fight, we cannot fit*, what bloody use are we,
But when we get to Berlin old Hitler he will say,
"Mein Gott, Mein Gott"
What a bloody fine lot are the boys of shiny 'C'"

**We were being trained as Fitters.*

The day after our arrival was spent queuing at the stores for uniforms along with culinary and other accessories. These accessories consisted of a white china pint mug, a knife fork and spoon, known as 'irons', a sewing kit, known as a 'housewife' and shoe brushes which had our service number stamped into them to shine our black leather boots. We were also issued with gas masks which were to be our constant companion. A small brass wheel, sewn onto the upper part of our sleeves, indicated that we were Aircraft Apprentices and a coloured hatband told the world which wing we belonged to, depending on the colour. As one may well imagine, the kitting out of six hundred boys took several days and many hours of queuing produced some poetic graffiti, like Milton's, "They also serve who only stand and wait"

After being kitted out, we were marched down the long winding hill to the workshops where we were issued with tool kits. The standard RAF tool kits consisted of a heavy wooden box approximately 2 ft. long and 1 ft. deep, containing a hand drill, a hammer, a screwdriver, a pair of pliers and anything else that one could acquire. Our training, ostensibly for three years, now began. Every morning we formed up on the parade ground and with overalls rolled under our arms, were marched down the hill to the workshops for lectures and practical work. Just one day a week was spent at the 'schools', a separate building, where we were taught technical subjects such as Mechanical Drawing, Metallurgy and The Theory of Flight. Interspaced with all this, 'square bashing', our disciplinary training, was an on going thing and it did nothing for our morale to be told that the whole disciplinary system was modelled on that of the Guards Brigade.

The last intake of boys to Halton had been in July 1939, the 40th entry. The system called for two entries per year, in January and July, but the outbreak of war had upset the programme resulting in a delay for our entry of three months. It was also part of the ritual for the boys to have three periods of leave a year, Easter, Summer and Christmas. As we had arrived at Halton on 10th March and Easter was in April, we had hardly settled in when we were off on Easter leave. The standard rate of pay for us boys was one shilling per day. However, of the seven shillings per week, four shillings was deferred, that is it was held back and paid to us when we went on leave. As there had been few paydays since joining, we all went off with a railway warrant, ten days ration allowance and a few shillings spending money.

I was not yet eighteen and had no parents in the country. It was, therefore necessary for me to have a guardian. My Aunt Mabel was appointed, and she lived in Manchester along with her husband, Uncle Cyril and daughter, Cousin Pam, and it was there that I went on my first leave.

This was the period known as the 'Phoney War'. The opening weeks of the war saw the over run of Poland and the Battle of the River Plate in which the German 'Pocket Battleship' Graf Spea was trapped and scuttled. Apart from that, nothing of note seemed to have happened and discounting the blackout and a little bit of food rationing, life seemed to go on much as it had done before the war.

HALTON

Only the better off were car owners and there was still a ration of petrol for 'pleasure motoring.' This was many years before motoring had become a nightmare of logjams. My uncle Cyril held an executive post with the L.E.C. (Lancashire Electric Co.) and the highlight of my leave was a drive out in his car to Buxton, a small spa town in the Pennines, about 30 miles from Manchester. We little realised, during these halcyon days, how close we were to the world shattering events that were to follow.

On our return to Halton the monotony of our training resumed and even when we read in the newspapers that the Germans had invaded Denmark and Norway, it seemed too remote to be real.

One day I fell foul of the squadron bully. He was several inches taller than me with a fairly athletic build and always accompanied by a small entourage of cronies. He was marching directly behind me on our return to the barracks and continuously tried to trip me. When I turned and objected he challenged me to settle the dispute on 'Bull-Back Field'. This was a grassy knoll between the barracks and the wooded hillside where traditionally all duals were fought. I accepted his challenge and that evening, at the appointed time, we met and prepared for a bare-knuckle fight. I never supposed that I could better him but I was determined to go down fighting. It wasn't long before his superior size and strength became apparent and at the first sign of my distress he himself called off the contest, helped me off the ground, and shook my hand. Halton seemed to have an edifying effect on its incumbents. Some six years later I met him again in the Sergeant's Mess at RAF Changi, Singapore. There we got a little drunk together like long lost friends.

It was very shortly after it became apparent that the battle of Norway had been lost, that the Germans launched their full scale 'Blitzkrieg' against France and the Low Countries. The whole nation waited with breath taking anxiety as the British Army was gradually squeezed into a tiny bridgehead around Dunkirk. The miracle evacuation proceeded and some three hundred and fifty thousand men were landed in England and had to be housed. These events galvanised the Halton authorities into action. The 38th and 39th entries, who were nearing the end of their training, were hurriedly passed out into 'man service'. The 40th entry took over No. 2 wing while our entry, the 41st, moved across the parade ground to No. 1 Wing, retaining the same squadron formations. This left Nos. 3 and 4 Wing barrack blocks empty for some of the returning troops.

Our new location, in number one wing, had certain advantages. Being right alongside the wooded hillside allowed us to surreptitiously disappear into the woods whenever we wanted to avoid our least favourite activities such as 'arms bend and stretch' under the direction of a P.T.I. (Physical Training Instructor). At that time there was a popular film going the rounds entitled, "Gold is where you find it", in which the leading character looks into the hills and says, "There's gold in them there hills." Parodying this, my friends would jokingly allege that the PTI, noticing my absence, would look towards the hills and say, "There's Gould in them there hills".

Unaccountably, the surname 'Gould' was uncommon at the time and I was quite surprised to meet a W.A.A.F. (Women's Auxiliary Air Force) with the same surname as mine. It was a strict rule that boys should not be seen to be accompanied by a female within camp bounds unless she was a close relative. At the same time the SP's (Service Police) were always on the lookout for rule breakers, no matter how trivial, to help meet their quota of charges. The temptation to bait them was too much for us, and we constantly walked about together in the hopes of being challenged. We would then produce our identity cards and claim to be brother and sister. The opportunity never came, however, and not being mutually attracted, we soon tired of it and abandoned the practice.

The tempo of war was now speeding up and the Battle of Britain was in full swing. To add incentive to our basic workshop training of filing metals to fine tolerances, we were told that the fighter squadrons were in need of tools and that our training work would be the production of spanners from a square of solid steel plate. We accepted this without question and worked hard to produce the best possible result. Some weeks later though, we heard of a load of spanners being tipped into the scrap bin.

It was now time for our summer leave which was also compressed from three weeks to ten days. Before I left home I was given a number of addresses of my parent's friends and relations who I promised to visit. I decided to spend my ten days with the Miles family who had a flat in Twickenham. Mrs. Miles was a life long friend of my mother's. Their children were all adult and scattered far and wide. Jean, the youngest, and a peer of my elder sister Joan, still lived at home awaiting her call up to the forces. Her fiancé, a soldier whom she had met in India, had been taken prisoner at Dunkirk and spent the rest of the war in a German POW camp. Jean was my constant companion during my leave when I also met a number of her attractive female friends. Unfortunately, having lived all my life in a single sex environment, I was unused to young girls and felt ill at ease in their company. I managed to overcome this handicap in the years to come.

By now hitchhiking by servicemen in uniform had become standard practice and it was possible to travel almost anywhere in the country for nothing. In the early autumn Jean Miles had been called up and was enlisted in the A.T.S. (Auxiliary Territorial Army). She was stationed at Bournemouth and on impulse, I persuaded a friend to accompany me on a visit to this popular seaside resort on a weekend pass. We had no difficulty in hitchhiking our way there but left it rather late in the day to start the return journey. By the time we reached the northern extremity of Oxford, the light was fading fast and so were our hopes of getting a lift to Aylesbury.

Eventually we abandoned the attempt and started to walk. The route from Oxford to Aylesbury involved a number of different roads and unfortunately for us there were no signposts. All signposts, throughout the country, had been removed with the invasion scare during the Battle of Britain, so we pressed on asking directions from anyone we met. By midnight the roads were deserted and we had to rely on guesswork. In the early hours, while crossing a railway line, we noticed a lighted building a mile or so down the track. It proved to be a signal box and as by then, we were totally lost, we started to make our way towards it. The signalman gave us directions and we returned to the road bridge where we sat on the parapet for a short rest. I immediately dozed off and almost fell from the parapet.

We struggled on through the rest of the night and walked into Aylesbury at dawn. We caught the first train to Wendover and walked the last mile to the guardroom where we were put on a charge for being absent without leave for eight hours. Later that day we were wheeled in front of the CO (Commanding Officer) and charged with the offence. We told our story of suffering and perseverance with good intent but the CO seemed quite unimpressed. "Seven days CC (Confined to Camp) and one days pay stopped". He announced the sentence with callous indifference, and we were led away to start our "jankers", as it was called.

The Battle of Britain ended in the middle of September and the planned German invasion abandoned. Because their losses were unsustainable, the Germans ceased daylight operations and turned to night bombing instead. This was the era of the "Blitz" and the Londoners were the first victims. German targets soon spread over the rest of the country and the name "Coventry" became synonymous with total devastation. One weekend I was invited by a colleague to his home in the little Huntingdonshire village of Warboys. On our Sunday evening return by bus we were half way between Luton and Aylesbury when we were brought to a halt by an air raid warning. The bus pulled off the road, switched off all lights, and waited. I had grave fears of another "seven days CC and one days pay stopped". Fortunately, the all clear went and we continued our journey in time to meet our deadline.

We had all enjoyed the long hot summer, especially the boys from India. Now the weather was turning uncomfortably cold as we began to experience our first English winter. Every morning brought the same routine. Dead on 6.30am a trumpeter would sound revalie and this would be followed by a PTI bursting into the barrack room shouting, "Wakey, wakey, Rise and shine, Come on lets be'avin ya, Feet on the deck". At once the scene was all action. Get washed and dressed, fold up our bed spaces, finish our room jobs and get out on the parade ground for ten minutes P.T. (Physical Training) before breakfast. After breakfast we formed up on the square for the long march down to the workshops. The forming up process seemed endless and being stationary and the weather cold, my hands and feet invariable became painfully numb.

Eventually it was time for Christmas leave and this time I returned to my Aunt in Manchester. Shortly after Easter my uncle Cyril had 'joined up' and received a commission in the Army. He was stationed in Edinburgh, where he was fortunate enough to be billeted with a Scottish family in their home but not fortunate enough to get Christmas leave. He did, however, send us a turkey which we never received. We believed it got buried under a pile of rubble in the heavily bombed Manchester Piccadilly station.

The German bombers were concentrating on Manchester at that time and the long, dark winter nights gave them ample opportunity. We did not have an air raid shelter but, being a ground floor flat, we had access to the underground cellar. The three of us, Aunt Mabel, Cousin Pam and myself surveyed the cellar with particular reference to the gas and water pipes contained within. We decided that, if the building was demolished, we would be trapped and either gassed or drowned. Consequently we were all agreed that, if we stayed in the flat and were killed, it was likely to be a quick death. This then was what we decided to do.

Before midnight the Air Raid Sirens sounded and shortly after, the dull thud of bombs exploding in the distance. To keep ourselves distracted we sat around the dining table and played 'Monopoly' while the house shook with the force of bombs exploding all around us. If we had been Muslims we would have said, "Allah was with us" for even after enduring the ordeal for several days, neither the house nor any of the three of us had received a scratch. In the morning we went out and watched, helplessly but sympathetically, the string of hollow faced families pushing prams containing the pitifully few possessions that they had managed to salvage from the ruins of their homes.

In the spring of 1940, shortly before France surrendered, the Italians, under Mussolini, had declared war on Britain and France hoping for easy pickings as a partner of Germany. They had a large Army in Libya but General Wavell, with some three Divisions defending Egypt, was more than able to hold them at bay. In order to demonstrate their military prowess the Italians decided to invade the small, primitive country of Albania. Greece came to the aid of their Albanian neighbours and a war of attrition ensued. Hitler could not tolerate this distraction to his grand strategy, the conquest of the Soviet Union, and so the German Army carried out a "Balkan Blitzkrieg", going through Yugoslavia, Albania and into Greece. General Wavell then detached as many men as he could afford to help the Greeks but it was a losing battle and they soon fell back on the island of Crete which the Germans then captured with paratroops.

These were the events that occupied the European stage in the early spring of 1941 and which later proved to have such a decisive effect on the Soviet campaign because it resulted in a postponement of "Operation Barbarosa", the invasion of the Soviet Union, which prevented the Germans from reaching Moscow before the Russian winter took them in its grip. Meanwhile the night bombing of Britain continued with the civilian population adapting to it in a number of ways. The London Tube station platforms became communal dormitories for those without air-raid shelters and the cockney sense of humour helped sustain their morale. A typical example was a family heading for their shelter when the mother wanted to return for her dentures.

"It's bombs they're dropping," said her husband "not bloody sandwiches."

Meanwhile our training at Halton continued apace with the subjects becoming much more varied than the initial basic filing. As we were expected to encounter aircraft of all vintages our training included such subjects as carpentry and rope splicing. Our RAF instructors were fond of reminding us that the planes were made of wood and the men of steel. They invariably added, "I joined the Service when Pontious was a Pilot (Pilate)". It was now a year since we first arrived at Halton, and I thought back about the words of Mr. Serdival in the school library, "And they'll be the best twelve years of your life". So far they had been the worst twelve months of my life. We were all looking forward to Easter leave, in fact we lived for our leaves. A number of boys kept 'count down charts' headed "D.T.E.L." (Days to Easter Leave). 'S' & 'X' replaced the 'E' as summer and Xmas were next.

For my Easter leave I decided to visit my Father's aunt Ruth who lived in the Lozells area of Birmingham. The houses were old and attached to each other in a solid block from one street to the next with the front doors opening directly onto the pavement. Aunt Ruth was a widow but her granddaughter, also called Ruth, lived with her. Young Ruth was a buxom, lively girl in her twenties who worked as a post woman delivering mail. She was newly married and her husband Harry was in the Army abroad. She would frequently burst into a popular song, "I'm just wild about Harry and Harry's wild about me".

The highlight of my stay was a visit, by car, to a holiday bungalow on the banks of the river Severn, just outside Bridgenorth, in Shropshire. This property belonged to Aunt Ruth's daughter, Rose, and her husband and it was they who took us there for the day. I wondered how the petrol was acquired for the journey although he was in a reserved occupation which, no doubt, provided certain special facilities.

On other days, when she was off duty, young Ruth would take me to various places in Birmingham such as the Ice Rink, where I soon realised that my future did not lie in ice-skating. When on my own I would take myself off to the cinema, invariably the Lozells Picture House, about four hundred metres from the house. This was significant because, on a short visit during my summer leave, when I expressed my intention to revisit this cinema, I was told that it no longer existed. Since my last leave, it had received a direct hit with a bomb. The manager, who had been fire watching, had been killed. Nevertheless, I went and inspected the pile of rubble that still awaited clearance.

The next major event on the world stage was the launching of 'Operation Barbarossa', the German invasion of the Soviet Union. Winston Churchill, who had always been staunchly anti-communist, announced, "My enemy's enemy is my friend". The immediate benefit to Britain of this event was the end of the nightly bombing. In addition we now had a major ally. Apart from the occasional nuisance raid and later a spate of attacks on buildings of historic interest, known as the "Baedeker Raids," no further bombing was experienced until the 'V1s & V2s' in 1944. The name 'Baedeker' referred to a German directory of historic buildings.

It was about this time that I developed an interest in photography as a hobby and joined the station photography club. The centre was well equipped with the means to produce prints, enlargements etc. I also became friendly with a 'naval air cadet' The Royal Navy also had apprentices who shared all our facilities, except that they were not allowed to go out of camp at any time they chose. They had to wait for the 'Liberty Boat,' which 'sailed' every half hour. This was to get them used to being at sea and consisted of those wishing to 'go ashore' forming a squad, at the appointed time, and being marched to the main gate where they 'stepped ashore.'

Shortly before our summer leave was due, my naval friend started to interest me in a 'blind date.' His girlfriend had a friend who was unattached and he arranged for the two of them to meet us at Baker Street Station at the start of our summer leave when we were to spend the rest of the day together. When we emerged from the station and I saw them, I was appalled. One was almost six feet tall and extremely thin while the other was about four foot ten and rather plump. Neither was particularly attractive. The tall one suited my friend who was about the same height while I was left with the plump one. I couldn't think of an excuse to get away, so I just said, "Well I've got to go. It was nice meeting you" and disappeared as fast as I could. That was the first and last time that I ever went on a 'blind date.' For my summer leave I decided to do a tour. A week in Twickenham, a week in Manchester and a week in Birmingham. I hitchhiked between the three venues being careful to start early and get to my destination before dark. I did not wish to repeat the trauma of the all night walk.

It was about this time that, back at Halton, I had a slight industrial accident. I was drilling a piece of steel on the power drill without wearing protective goggles. A minute piece of hot metal struck my eyeball. It was not overly painful at first but I went on sick parade the following morning and was proscribed M&D (Medicine and Duties). Sick parade was at the same time as morning PT and all those not excused duties were expected to attend a PT session in the evening. This I failed to do and received seven days 'jankers' as a result. However, I reported sick again the next morning and this time the M.O. (Medical Officer) referred me to the large military hospital that was part of the Halton complex. I spent ten days there with a bandaged eye in the company of Pilots who had been burned and blinded in combat.

On the 7th December 1941, the world received the stupendous news that the Japanese had attacked the American base at Pearl Harbour and that the Germans had declared war on the US. We had always confidently believed that we would win the war but we didn't know how. Now we knew how!

Halton was possessed of excellent sporting facilities and the one that I found that I most excelled at, was swimming. In my last full year in school I received the challenge cup for the

Junior Swimming Championship so I decided to concentrate on this sport. I soon found myself a member of the station swimming team, membership of which enjoyed certain concessions to allow for nightly training. I teamed up with a boy named Harrison because he and I were exactly equal. When competing against each other we seemed to take it in turns to win. Most of all we enjoyed the supper after the training sessions which included a pint of cold milk, my favourite drink. This was particularly appreciated because it was the only drink, other than water, that I ever had on the camp. The cookhouse tea was always sweetened and so was the tea in the N.A.A.F.I. (Navy, Army, Air Force Institute). This was a government owned organisation to provide all catering and canteen facilities for the armed forces. My difficulties with the sweet tea were due to the fact that I was born with a condition known as 'Sucrose Intolerance'. My body lacked the enzymes necessary to convert Sucrose and Fructose into Glucose. As the digestive system starts in the mouth, anything with a sweet taste was immediately rejected. To me a sweet taste is repulsive.

Our main swimming contestants were the London Fire Service, who were full of praise, possibly with a little envy, for our facilities. Our baths were part of the workshops complex and enjoyed the same generous heating facilities. The Fire Service repeatedly complained that they could not get any fuel to heat their baths, which were in Battersea. On the return match at Battersea in February 1942, they met us with transport at Baker Street station and continued to complain about their lack of fuel. We put this down to 'gamesmanship' until we got to their baths where the water temperature was displayed in large figures. It was 39°F (4°C), the recommended temperature for fridges. "Thank heavens I'm only a reserve," I thought. But alas! my relief was short lived. I was told that I was to compete in the 100 yards free style. When the time came and I was standing on my starting block, I seemed to go into a hypnotic trance. I ignored the starter's "Go" and only the splash of the other swimmers hitting the water spurred me into action. I shall never forget the shock of hitting the water. My whole body went numb and even after swimming as hard as I could for the hundred yards, it was still numb when I clambered out.

By now we were nearing the end of our apprenticeship. It had been cut from three to two years to fuel the needs of the rapidly expanding RAF. One of the final phases was a month working on complete aeroplanes in an unheated hangar. It was mid February and the temperature was well below zero. Each morning started with us sitting on our toolboxes, in classroom formation, for an hour's technical lecture. I had great difficulty in concentrating on the lecture. All I could think of was the cold. I even looked at two old aircraft, a Hurricane and a Spitfire, standing nearby and thought, "You've been here all night, you must be absolutely frozen". They certainly looked it.

As soon as our passing-out date was announced, 25th. March, 1942, the 'days to' charts were changed to D.T.P.O. (Days To Passing Out). The excitement grew as we waited to hear to which RAF station we were to be posted. There was a certain amount of nostalgia as well, as we mentally said goodbye to the uniquely Haltonian expressions with obscure origins such as 'Snag'. A snag was a leading aircraft apprentice whose badge of rank was a single mini stripe. There was normally one for each barrack room. Another term was "Skate". A skate was a lad who was constantly in trouble usually for trivial things, like smoking, which was strictly forbidden and which usually warranted seven days jankers. A rumour was current that skates were named after the fish which has a small brain. We felt glad to miss the PTI's (Physical Training Instructors) who were our constant disciplinarians and who were regarded with little affection. The only exception to this was Eddy Phillips, a well known pre-war heavy weight boxer who, with his cauliflower ears and battered face, was as soft as putty.

Finally the great day arrived. It was celebrated with a formal parade and a few speeches. Had it been known at the time, this would have included a statement that Sir Frank Whittle, inventor of the jet engine, had at one time been an aircraft apprentice at Halton, which was considered the Eton or Harrow of the RAF.

After the parade we were given our postings. Coincidentally, I was paired with Des Cheverton, one of the military schoolboys from India always referred to as Chevy'. We were both posted to No. 58 M.U. (Maintenance Unit) at Newark, in Nottinghamshire, where we became close friends.

4
GROUND STAFF

No. 58 MU was a small maintenance unit on the outskirts of Newark. It looked more like a scrap yard than a RAF unit except that most of the scrap lying about was aircraft parts. On our arrival, Chevy and I reported to the orderly room where we were given an address in the town and told that this was where we would be billeted. On locating the address we found it occupied by a large, motherly woman of middle age who welcomed us in and showed us to a bedroom with two single beds which was to be ours. We could not believe our good fortune. After the rigours of Halton it seemed too good to be true. With our landlady cooking our meals and washing our clothes, it was like being in 'Civy Street'.

The next morning we reported to the Engineering Officer where we were brought back to reality. The unit was divided between salvage and repair. Those on salvage would go off for days on end to salvage any crashed aircraft in a large area of the Midlands and East Anglia. Those on repairs would be temporarily based on a nearby operational airfield to give assistance, where necessary, to those employed on servicing and repair of operational aircraft. On learning that we were straight out of Halton the Engineering Officer had no hesitation in placing us in the repair section, and promptly drove us round to our billet in the town to collect 'our kit'. This was in fact all our worldly possessions which were contained in a 'kit bag.' He then drove us to RAF Wadington, a bomber station a few miles south of Lincoln, where he left us in the charge of the servicing 'Chiefy.' The 'Chiefy' was the flight- Sergeant in control of aircraft servicing. The RAF had been formed in 1918 out of the Royal Flying Core and the Royal Naval Air Service but most of the inherited traditions came from the Navy. The naval rank equivalent to flight-Sergeant was chief Petty Officer, who was always referred to as 'Chiefy', hence the flight-Sergeant's sobriquet.

Waddington was one of the first stations to receive the new Lancaster bombers. The station's compliment of aircraft was a mixture of Hampdens, Manchesters and Lancasters. The Manchester was the forerunner of the Lancaster, with only two engines, which were Rolls Royce 'Vultures' with 24 cylinders set in an X profile and driving a seventeen ft. diameter propeller. The Hampdens were still the only aircraft that were operating regularly. As it was early spring and the country was on double summer time, darkness fell about bedtime. This was the time that the Hampdens usually took-off and as our billet was an ex married quarters house located off the end of the main runway, we found our sleep

GROUND STAFF

somewhat disturbed by the heavily laden aircraft struggling to gain height directly above us.

Within a week of our arrival the Engineering Officer returned and told us that he was transferring us to Coningsby, some 40 miles away, near Boston. This turned out to be an almost prophetic move. Unknown to us, at the same time as we were travelling, twelve Lancasters, six from Waddington and six from Coningsby, were taking part in a low level daylight attack on a ball bearing factory in Augsburg returning in darkness.

None of the six Waddington Lancasters returned to base. There was, however, one survivor, Squadron Leader Nettleton, the leader of the operation, who managed to crash-land his plane at RAF Squires Gate, near Blackpool and was later awarded the Victoria Cross. Coningsby received back four out of their six Lancasters. They were full of holes some as big as footballs. This then was the scene that we were confronted with the next morning when we arrived for work at the servicing area. I thought as I looked at it, "Halton never prepared us for this". Not surprisingly, we soon heard that we were not to attempt the repairs, as a team of technicians was on its way from Avro, the manufacturers who, with their specialist knowledge, experience and replacement parts, would soon have the work done. This was the last daylight operation carried out by Lancasters until the summer of 1944, when the allies had achieved complete air supremacy.

We spent the next ten weeks or so augmenting the servicing

staff of 97 squadron as more new Lancasters started to arrive from the factory. As these aircraft were new, they required less attention than the older Hampdens, and we began to feel somewhat under employed. The authorities felt the same way and in the middle of June, we were returned to Newark to await a decision on our future. The next couple of weeks were like a holiday. We enjoyed living and being waited on in our 'civy digs' and with little to do, we sometimes went swimming in the river Trent which, in those days, was relatively unpolluted. Then our posting came through. It was to No. 226 MU at Glengormley, a suburb of Belfast in Northern Ireland.

No. 226 MU was another salvage and repair unit. It consisted of a small hutted camp in the then rural suburb of Glengormley. The camp had sufficient accommodation for most of its incumbents but a few, mostly Officers, who were in a position to arrange things, were accommodated in 'civy digs'. The station adjutant was one of these and it became talk of the camp, that on returning to his 'digs' one day, he was greeted by his landlady with, "So you're posted then?" He had found this hard to believe, for although he was at the centre of communications, he himself had not heard of this, and was shocked to later find that it was true. So much for security on camp.

No. 226 was unique among MUs in that its stores contained a range of civilian clothes and its vehicles had their RAF markings painted out. This was because, whenever an allied plane crashed in the Republic, or the 'Free State' as it was

GROUND STAFF

known then, a salvage party dressed in civilian clothes and riding in unmarked vehicles would, by arrangement with the Irish government, go and salvage it. They would then return it to the north. One of these was a 'Mitchell', an American medium bomber, which had attempted to fly the Atlantic with overload tanks and run into trouble. It had crash-landed but was considered repairable. As a result it was taken to RAF Aldagrove, now Belfast Airport, to be repaired by our repair section. More on this later.

Whilst awaiting a repair slot, somewhere in Northern Ireland, and curious to know more of the salvage section's work, I managed to accompany a survey party that was to inspect a crash site in the Mountains of Mourne, in County Down. This was rough terrain and the vehicle could get no less than 2 miles from the crash. It was a hard, uphill trek to our destination where we found a woeful sight. A severely damaged Spitfire, in the cockpit of which, we found ample evidence to suggest that the Pilot had been on board and had lost his life.

Soon after, Chevy and I were sent on permanent detachment to RAF Aldagrove, on the banks of Loch Neagh, to join the unit's repair party who were already there. The party consisted of some twenty or so Fitters and Mechanics, who were all housed in one big wooden hut. They were from various parts. A few from the Free State who had volunteered to serve in the British armed forces for the duration of the war. Others were from Northern Ireland. The rest were from Great Britain. We soon all formed a common bond.

Our first job was in a hangar on the far side of the airfield where we found the 'Mitchell' bomber, referred to earlier. Our task was to restore it to its former glory. After weeks of work with our rudimentary tool kits, it appeared to look very little different. Then one morning the cry went up, "The Yanks are coming". Seven months after Pearl Harbour, the Americans were starting to arrive in Britain, the advanced guard to Northern Ireland. Soon the cry was, "They're here" as, with a squeal of brakes, two American trucks pulled up outside the hangar. Out jumped a number of men in civilian clothes. They off loaded a number of expensive looking metal cabinets on castors and wheeled them into the hangar. When they opened the cabinet doors we looked in amazement at rows of highly polished chromium plated ring spanners, socket sets and other sophisticated tools that we had never before seen in our lives. The appearance of the bomber had changed more by the end of the day, than it had in the weeks that we had been working on it. Wisely it was decided to leave them to it.

We returned to the main servicing hangar where a Lockheed Hudson, maritime reconnaissance plane, was being prepared for air-test. I managed to talk my way on board as a passenger and enjoyed my first experience of flying. For my next, I had to work hard. We were doing a major overhaul on a 'Wellington' bomber. The Wellington was of a previous generation design and consisted of a metal framework covered by 'doped' fabric. The framework was of 'Geodetic' construction, a unique principle invented by Dr. Barnes Wallace of 'Bouncing Bomb' fame. It had first been used on the giant airships R100 and R101. My job was to strip off all the dope from the fabric, using solvents. Then brush on a fresh application of red dope, which tightened and preserved the fabric. Finally re-spraying the camouflage. I felt I had earned my place on the air test.

There was an anxious moment while I was cleaning the spray gun by spraying petrol into an empty space in the hangar. One of my colleagues walked through the cloud of petrol vapour with a lighted cigarette. I held my breath because the result could be horrendous, yet nothing happened. Either the cigarette wasn't hot enough to light the fuel or the petrol to air ratio was too weak to ignite. I never learned which, but was careful to avoid a repetition.

Although I was still friendly with Chevy, I found myself also drawn to an Irish colleague named Paddy Boyle mainly because of his cavalier attitude to life and because he made me laugh. Somehow he had managed to get himself a reputation for being a 'lecher.' A séance was held in our hut one night and when we were invited to ask the spirit a question, Paddy said, "Are you a woman?" This caused an outburst of laughter which broke up the séance.

Pay parade, in the RAF, consisted of an airman from the accounts department with a big ledger and an Officer with a bag of money. Both were sat at a table with their eyes fixed on what they were doing. The parade was assembled in rows facing them. The airman with the ledger would call out a name and the person whose name was called would answer, "Sir, 124" or what ever the last three digits of his service number were. Then the ledger-man would call out an amount in sterling which the Officer would count out. The payee would then march briskly up to the table, give a smart salute, and pick up the money. Paddy always reckoned that the paying out duo were so engrossed in what they were doing that they were oblivious to anything else. One pay parade he decided to prove it. When his name was called, he answered, "Sir! knife, fork, spoon", then sauntered up to the table and with a salute that looked more like an Indian beggar's salaam, picked up his pay and sauntered off. He was right. Apart from a few sniggers in the ranks, nothing changed.

One day I was walking along a road on the camp, when a staff-car pulled up and a voice said, "Jump in". It was Paddy, alone and in the driving seat. "Where did you get this?" I asked. "I just borrowed it from the M.T." (Motor Transport), he replied. "Come on we're going for a drive." We drove around for about half an hour and then headed for the M.T. Section. He parked the car and we both walked off. On another occasion he was giving me a lift to the hangar on a pushbike, with me on the cross bar, when we saw ahead of us, the Station Warrant Officer. Like most SWO's. who were responsible for discipline, he was a bit of a Martinet. With total unconcern Paddy steered the bike towards the hangar door, jumped off and gave the bike a push, leaving me to coast into the hangar on the cross bar while he continued to walk along the road. When he came abreast of the SWO and was challenged about the bicycle, he casually replied,

"What bicycle?" When the SWO looked in the hangar all he saw was me, working at a bench, and no bicycle. Without the evidence he was powerless to take the matter any further.

Paddy was a Catholic and lived in the Falls road, though this address had little significance for me at the time. He always seemed reluctant to take me to his home and I wondered why. Eventually I found out. He had to go into hospital in Belfast and whilst visiting him, I met his sister and her father, who was a widower. They took me home with them for a cup of tea. The house was sparsely furnished and seemed to have seen better days. Obviously they were not well off and Paddy seemed reluctant to admit this, to me at any rate.

Another colleague, with whom I became friendly, was Jeff. I'm not sure that I ever knew his first name, as he was always known as Jeff, because his surname was Jeffries. Jeff, like us, was an 'ex brat' as all ex Halton boys were known. He was in the 40th entry, the one before us. He had applied to become a Flight Engineer and was awaiting his 'boards' (a series of tests and interviews) and his subsequent call up. In due course these came to fruition and he departed with our good wishes for RAF St. Athan, the training centre for Flight Engineers.

We never heard from Jeff again but we certainly did hear of him. Some three or four months after he left us, the Press and News Reels were headlining an event which they were describing as "The bravest deed of the war". A New Zealand Pilot, flying a Stirling heavy bomber on a mission to Milan, in Northern Italy, had been badly shot up on their way to the target and the Pilot himself had been almost mortally wounded. Nevertheless they pressed on, bombed the target and headed back for base. They crossed the English coast with only a few minutes petrol left in their tanks. The Pilot ordered his crew to bail out as he himself intended to ditch the plane in the sea off the coast. Four of the crew obeyed, and parachuted to safety. The Flight Engineer and the Bomb Aimer refused to leave him. They decided to stay and help him ditch the plane. In the event all three were killed. The Flight Engineer was Sergeant Jeffries. Knowing Jeff, we all believed that he had taken over the controls but lacked the skill to make a successful ditching.

The Pilot was awarded a posthumous V.C. and a letter from Jeff's mother told us that she had received a personal letter from Air Chief Marshal Sir Arthur Harris, C. in C. Bomber Command, stating that her son had a full part in what the press were calling 'the bravest deed of the war,' but that the award always went to the Captain.

This news served only to strengthen my determination to follow in Jeff's footsteps and I put in my application to become a Flight Engineer. Besides, I would become a full-time flyer, which had always been my ultimate aim. I then started the long wait for my boards and the even longer wait for my call to arms.

It was about this time that we had a visit from one of our unit's salvage teams. An American 'Flying Fortress' bomber had strayed off the solid perimeter track and one of its main wheels had sunk into the soft soil adjacent. The team were busy jacking it up onto a tracked bogey, prior to pulling it out of the mire, when a small team of American soldiers arrived with a 10,000 gallon petrol bowser. "You don't want to bother with that", they said, "Here, tie this round the leg" and they tossed our men a steel hawser. The other end they attached to the bowser. "Take it away", was the cry. The cable came taught and the undercarriage came off, leaving our crew with a real salvage job. The Americans just left us to it.

I had always had in mind a weekend visit to Dublin, which was permitted provided one wore civilian clothes. I did not have any civilian clothes but our unit stores did and this is what I intended. Unfortunately, before my plans could come to fruition, an order was promulgated stating that, because of the security risk, no further visits to the Free State would be sanctioned. The exception to this of course was those Irish boys whose homes were in the Free State. Apparently it had been discovered that the Germans had been chatting up our servicemen in the pubs after plying them with drinks.

Now my turn came for the Flight Engineer's board. I spent a couple of days in Belfast being medically examined, interviewed and educationally tested. My status as an 'ex brat' stood me in good stead for the interviews and the educational tests were not hard. However, when it came to general knowledge, I was appalled at my own ignorance. I did not know the name of a single artist. It was then that I realised how narrow my formal education had been and I was determined to start a course of self-education which has been on-going all my life.

The NAAFI at Aldagrove had competition from the Salvation Army which also had a canteen on the camp. The 'Sally Anne' offered a better menu and I could get tea without sugar so most evenings a group of us would foregather there to chat and while away the time. The group often included WAAFs, when a little bit of paring would sometimes take place. On a particular occasion, one of the girls seemed to take a special interest in me. She was auburn haired and not unattractive. When it got around dusk, she suggested a walk. I acquiesced. We walked across a field until we came to a haystack. She suggested we might relax in the straw. Again I acquiesced. I knew what was expected of me but I had a problem. I was halfway through a course of treatment for scabies, which I had caught from my blankets, which were only fumigated when a case came to light. Gone was the luxury of sheets that we enjoyed at Halton. Now we slept between hairy blankets. I felt that close contact between us may well infect her and I didn't feel that I could risk that. So I did nothing. There were limits to the extent to which she would lead me and we soon returned to the camp. I knew that I should have explained things to her but I felt too ashamed. Ever after she would not speak to me. A case of 'woman scorned' syndrome, I thought.

The standard leave cycle for the armed forces based in Great Britain was seven days every three months. Except for those with homes in Ireland, it was fourteen days every six months, because of the travelling involved. I had now been in Northern Ireland six months and my first leave was due. I planned to spend it with Aunt Mabel, or Mel, as she preferred to be called, and Pam. Their situation had changed considerably in the last twelve months or so. They no longer lived in Manchester. Uncle Cyril, in his 'civy digs' in Edinburgh, had fallen in love with his landlady's daughter and had asked Aunt Mel for a divorce. In those days adultery was the main reason for divorce and as the case was not contested, it was settled fairly speedily and without too much heartache.

Under the 'Direction of Labour' law, those between eighteen and sixty years of age, who were not in the armed forces or in a reserved occupation, were directed into some sort of war work. A number of young girls opted for the 'Land Army', where they worked on farms, conspicuous by their uniforms of fawn riding-britches and bright green sweaters. Aunt Mel chose to work in a munitions factory. Scattered around the country, mostly in rural areas, were 'Shadow Factories' which were extensions of the major plants in the industrial areas. She was sent to a shadow factory in Burnham-on-Sea, in Somerset and as Pam was still under eighteen and a dependant, Pam went with her. They lived in a boarding house in neighbouring Bridgwater. There was room for me on a temporary basis so that is where I headed in mid-December, 1942.

It was a long, tedious journey. First I had to call at our unit at Glengormley to collect the necessary documentation.

Then into Belfast to catch the boat train to Larne. Larne to Stranraer, in Scotland, a distance of about 35 miles, was the shortest sea crossing and the one invariably used, though when we first came to Ireland, we sailed all night between Liverpool and Belfast. The crossing, in the late afternoon, took about two hours. There was quite a swell and the ship was pitching and rolling causing a bit of seasickness. Two soldiers, standing a few feet apart against the ship's rail, were being violently sick and the wind was blowing the vomit of one into the face of the other. The fact that the one on the receiving end was making no effort to avoid it made me realise just how dreadful sea-sickness must feel and how lucky I was that I had never experienced any form of travel sickness, even in the most extreme circumstances.

The train journey from Stranraer to London took all night. Then from London to Bristol a stopping train to Bridgewater arrived in the early afternoon, twenty-four hours after leaving Glengormley. As long as it now takes to travel by air from the UK to Australia. The winter of 1942/43 proved to be the mildest that I can ever remember, for which I was eternally grateful as it turned out to be the only winter in my working life that I earned my living by working with my hands often in the open or in unheated buildings. Cold has always been an anathema to me. Because of the mild conditions I was able to enjoy much of my leave in the open cycling with Pam in the nearby Quantock hills during Christmas week. One morning at breakfast I was telling Pam and her mother that I had dreamt, during the night, that I fell out of bed and woke up to find myself on the floor by the bed. Pam laughed and

GROUND STAFF

said, "I wondered what that loud bang was in the middle of the night".

We had now come to the end of the third year of the war which had started with the country's fortunes at their lowest ebb. The loss of most of our Far East possessions, the surrender of Singapore and its garrison and the Japanese poised to invade India and Australia. The Germans renewing their onslaught on the Soviet Union and threatening the invasion of Egypt and the Middle East. It ended with two decisive allied victories, the siege of Stalingrad and the break through at El Alamein under General Montgomery which Churchill described as, "Not the beginning of the end but, at least, the end of the beginning". The Americans, in the Pacific also, were beginning to contain the Japanese advance.

My return to duty involved the same dreary 24 hour journey. I could certainly see why the authorities only wished this on us once every six months. I didn't realise it at the time but I was about to make the journey back to England yet again, joining a road convoy that required me as an aircraft technician to accompany a badly damaged Wellington Bomber to a civilian maintenance unit at Roade, in Northamptonshire. The final leg back to Ireland, proved to be the most tedious of all as we zig-zagged consignments from one location to the next, painfully working our way to Stranraer for the final crossing home.

5
LEARNING TO FLY

Towards the end of April orders came for me to start my training as a Flight Engineer and once again I did the long trek this time to South Wales. I was heading for No. 4 S of TT at St. Athan, about 15 miles west of Cardiff. The letters S of TT stood for 'School of Technical Training', (Halton being No. 1). With the loss of Singapore, St. Athan was reputed to be the biggest RAF base in the world. In addition to technical training facilities to match Halton, it consisted of a large maintenance and repair unit and a full size airfield with runways. The accommodation for trainees, however, consisted merely of rows of wooden huts linked together by covered walkways.

Having arrived from Ireland on my own, I now had to make new friends. There must be a quality of the Irish that draws me to them. I soon found myself developing a special friendship with an Anglo-Irishman named Paddy Curtis. His father had been a regular soldier in the Irish Guards and had married a First World War widow from Guernsey. Their home was in Torquay. Paddy didn't amuse me like my friend in Ireland but he did have the same relaxed attitude to life. He was also an ex Halton apprentice of the same entry as Jeff.

It was now some eight months since Jeff had gone from Northern Ireland to train as a Flight Engineer. At that time Flight Engineers were urgently needed to join the crews of the new four engined heavy bombers that were rapidly coming into service. Flight Engineers were only recruited from the aircraft technicians of ground crew. Jeff was an Engine Fitter and because of the urgency, his time at St. Athan only lasted six weeks. Our intake, however, were all airframes qualified, and it was thought necessary for us to have a good grounding on engines. Consequently our course was scheduled to last five months.

The training was much like Halton except that there was no practical work. We sat around in small groups in the workshops complex listening to lectures, with one day a week in a classroom. Because of the lack of physical activity, the authorities thought it necessary for each day to contain a period of physical training. This consisted of the tiresome 'arms bend and stretch' under the direction of the hated PTI's. A number of us had other ideas. Because we were involved in more strenuous sports out of working hours, we considered the PT sessions unnecessarily tedious. Thus started a five month long battle of wits between the anti PT faction

LEARNING TO FLY

and the authorities. Each time we found a way of evading the sessions the authorities would change the system.

First, the PT was held during the morning break. Asking to go to the loo just before break time, we returned too late for it. This was met with a restriction on visits to the loo half an hour before break time. Our reply to this was ingenious. We each obtained an armband containing a pair of Corporal's stripes. Most of the instructors were Corporals. When the break signal sounded, we slipped on our stripes and walked around pretending to be instructors. The next change was to reschedule the PT to the last fifteen minutes of the afternoon and to hold it in the very large Gymnasium to which we would be marched after lectures. There were two large doors to the gym both of which were open. As we marched into one and broke ranks we carried on walking and walked out of the other, then faded away. On one occasion, whilst walking away, we heard a shout behind us. We knew it was for us but daren't look round. Then we heard running footsteps so we started to run. We ran through the network of WAAF's huts where the PTI lacked the courage to follow.

In the educational classrooms, we had two very different instructors. One was a good psychologist, while the other had a weakness for teasing Scotsmen. The latter would talk about the flower of English youth being spent on the German cities with continual emphasis on the word 'English'. Eventually a voice would pipe up, "Wah aboot Scotelund?" "Scotland?" he would reply, "Ah yes, that far flung outpost of empire, the only objection to which being that it's not flung far enough."

We were attending a lesson with the other instructor, one warm afternoon immediately after a big meal, when he noticed my head start to nod and my eyes to droop. He stopped the lesson, came over to me, and said in a quiet voice, "If you feel sleepy put your head on the desk and have a nap, you'll feel better for it." I took his advice but to my surprise it seemed to awaken me and dispel the drowsiness.

The large workshop complex contained a well-equipped and warm swimming baths which I would often visit in the evenings. One evening, whilst in the water, I got talking to a girl and arranged to see her after our swim. When we got outside I hardly recognised her. She was wearing glasses and her WAAF uniform did nothing for her. The meeting was never repeated. On another occasion I was approached by a young man, acting as a sort of agent, and challenged to a swimming race against 'his boy,' as he called him. The race was arranged and took place that evening. I won by a comfortable margin. Nothing more was said and I was left wondering what it was all about.

In addition to the swimming baths, the workshop complex contained a theatre of reasonable proportions. Being such a large base, St. Athan attracted some first rate entertainers. In due course we had a visit from the Sadler Wells Opera Company whose base was Covent Garden. As admission was free and I had nothing better to do, I went along prepared to be thoroughly bored. To my great surprise I was held spellbound by the lovely arias in 'Madam Butterfly' and from then on I became a devotee of opera.

LEARNING TO FLY

The last month of the course was spent on 'type training'. This was when we specialised on a particular aircraft. If we had been left to choose, every body would have chosen 'Sunderland' flying boats because, doing U-boat patrols, they had the lowest casualty rate. Instead, the Sergeant in charge would announce an aircraft type and then a number. If one's service number ended with that digit, one joined the group specialising in that aircraft. When it came to the three heavy bombers, Lancaster, Halifax and Stirling, their popularity was in that order. When he called out, "Lancaster", Paddy and I held our breath for the numbers. "Four," he shouted. "That's me," I thought and joined the group assembling. A couple of numbers later I was pleased to see Paddy join the group as well.

Now that we were both on Lancasters we had a further choice, between Mark 1 and Mark 2. Mk.1s had liquid cooled Merlin engines while Mk.2s had air cooled Hercules. I had heard somewhere that, on test, a Hercules engine had continued to run at full power while being fired at by a machine gun. The Mk.2's the plane for us I thought. Half way through the month we had a technical test. The top so many would finish on Mk.2s. This provided a powerful incentive, and both Paddy and I worked hard studying and revising in the evenings

Midway through the month we spent a week at the Avro factory, near Stockport, Cheshire. In addition to seeing the Lancasters being built, we had technical lectures from a member of the design staff. I sat spellbound at the depth of his knowledge. He could switch effortlessly from the workings of the constant speed propeller to the intricacies of the automatic Pilot. I was reminded of a line from Goldsmith's Deserted Village, "and still the wonder grew, that one small head could carry all he knew."

The factory, being situated within a large town, provided a rare opportunity for us to expand our social life and every night saw us all out on the town. Ever since Dunkirk the only branch of the services that were in action against the enemy in the European theatre was the RAF aircrew and they were regarded by the other services as the 'Glamour Boys.' Second only to them were the aircrew under training, who were instantly recognisable by the white flash in their forage caps. Thus we had little difficulty in 'pulling the birds,' to the extent that one of our number, not of our immediate circle, managed to contract Gonorrhoea.

On our return to St. Athan with only two weeks to go we continued studying assiduously and at the final exam I found myself only two marks behind the one who was top of the entry. If I'd worked more and played less at the factory, I could have been top. It was then that I realised that I wasn't as 'thick' as I had always believed myself to be. I was just academically lazy.

From St. Athan Paddy and I were both posted to No. 1678 Conversion Unit at the aptly named RAF station, Little Snoring, in Norfolk. Little Snoring was a satellite of Fulsham and the conversion units were where the crews that had

LEARNING TO FLY

formed together at the O.T.Us. (Operational Training Units) were introduced to the four-engined heavy bombers that had now replaced all the old bombers. It was also where they were introduced to a new member of the crew, the Flight Engineer. We started flying as passengers on air experience flights in Lancaster Mk.2s. It soon became evident that the Lancaster Mk.2s were on their way out. We learned later that whatever the merits of the Hercules engines, they were not as highly developed as the Rolls Royce Merlins, and could only accept half the supercharger pressure, consequently the Mk.2s could not reach the same altitude as the Mk.1s. This made them more vulnerable and they were soon phased out.

Along with Paddy and me, two other lads had come to Little Snoring from St. Athan. Their surnames were Cosgrove and Wilson. Again we never knew their first names as they were always known as Cossey and Tug. One day, during this period of uncertainty, we were all four having a discussion on our chances of survival. Ever the pessimist, I said that I did not expect to survive unscathed. Cossey on the other hand declared, "Oh I reckon I'll get through." At the end of the war both Cossey and Tug were dead, Paddy was a prisoner of war, and I was the only one who survived unscathed.

Cossey was always a source of great amusement to us. One day he was telling us about an evening with his girlfriend. It was a cold night and they were walking along together. The girl mentioned that her hands were cold. "Put your hand in my pocket," he said indicating his trouser pocket, which she did. Then Cossey had a bright idea. He excused himself, went behind a bush and tore the pocket out of his trousers. Returning, he persuaded the girl to replace her hand in his pocket. "And there he was," he exclaimed, with obvious pride, "waiting for her."

It was about this time that I bought myself a ten-year-old B.S.A. motorcycle for £15. I proceeded to teach myself to ride it on the empty perimeter track of the airfield. I soon decided that I was proficient enough to ride into Norwich which allowed a companion and I to remain there after the last transport had left. That saved us the expense of a bed in the 'Toch-H', a charity similar to the Salvation Army. All driving tests had been suspended for the duration of the war and provisional licences, which could be obtained on application, entitled one to drive the same as a full licence. When driving tests were resumed after the war, if one had held a wartime provisional for three years, one could automatically obtain a full licence. Thus, ever since 1947, I have held a full driving licence without ever having taken a driving test.

The Lancaster Mk2 conversion unit now began running down and the aircraft were deployed elsewhere. This caused some initial confusion, and we were all transferred to RAF Oakington, a nearby airfield in Cambridgeshire to await our future. We all took the opportunity for a week's leave, which was due. The others all went home. For a change, I decided to visit the Isle of Mann where lived a girl who I had known at Halton. She had given me an open invitation. When I got there I was surprised to learn that she was married

LEARNING TO FLY 69

and heavily pregnant, though not necessarily in that order. Nevertheless I took the opportunity to explore the island. On my return I had a slight brush with the Service Police. By then the whole country had become rather blasé about the possibility of 'gas warfare,' and I had omitted to take my gas mask with me on leave. On approaching the dock area I was stopped by two S.Ps. and my details noted. On my return to Oakington, I found myself in front of the CO charged with separating myself from my gas mask. Of course I was now a Sergeant and as such could not be given 'jankers.' Instead I received a reprimand which had the same effect as water off a duck's back.

It was around Christmas, 1943 and the air offensive was gathering momentum. Night after night the heavy bombers were attacking Berlin, with considerable losses. General Montgomery's Alamein offensive had carried the eighth Army through to Tunisia, where they had met up with the American Army that had landed in Morocco and Algeria. Together they had crossed the Mediterranean and were locked in battle with the German Army in Italy.

Shortly before Christmas, orders came through for our posting to fresh conversion units. Paddy, Cossey and Tug went to Stradishall, in Suffolk while I went to Wratting Common, just over the border in Cambridgeshire. Both camps were five or six miles from the market town of Haverhill and we agreed to meet there on our days off.

Oakington to Wratting Common was a distance of about

twenty miles and I had my motorcycle to transfer, and hopefully to transport me. There were several things wrong with the machine. In addition to the lights needing attention the main sprocket had a row of about ten teeth missing which caused the chain to come off at the most awkward times. Having attached my kit bag firmly to the pillion seat, I set off in mid afternoon. It was late 1943 and with the clocks on 'summer time,' (double summer time in the summer) it was pitch-dark by five o'clock. It was also very cold. I continued to thread my way through the country lanes with virtually no illumination until the cold forced me to stop at a garage in the middle of a village. Here I bought a battery operated cycle lamp which I tied onto the headlamp with 'borrowed' string.

Unknown to me, a middle-aged woman had been watching me and now came over and spoke to me. "You look frozen," she said. "Why don't you come home with me and have a warm before you continue?" The offer was too good to refuse and she took me to her house nearby, where she lived alone, and placed me in front of a roaring fire. She also gave me a light meal, "to fortify me for the journey." I felt so grateful but didn't know how to repay her. Then I had an idea. "Would you accept my sweet coupons in appreciation for what you've done for me?" I asked. "No I couldn't possibly," she answered. When I explained to her that, because of my peculiar taste, they were of no use to me, she accepted them with gratitude.

So I continued my journey in pitch darkness. Though the

LEARNING TO FLY

cycle lamp did little to help me see where I was going, at least others would be able to see me. I managed to keep a steady 30 mph by using the telegraph poles to show me where the road was.

The conversion unit at Wratting Common was equipped with Stirlings which were being phased out of operational service and being replaced by Lancasters which had a greater ceiling height. The Stirlings served perfectly well for converting the crews onto four engined aircraft. I hadn't been on the base long before I found that I had a double. We were both Sergeant Flight Engineers, the only difference was that he was an instructor and I was a pupil. Before we were 'crewed up' that is, before we joined one of the existing six man crews that had come from OTU, we flew as passengers on 'cross-country' flights with crews under training. Sometimes these crews carried an instructor, referred to as a screen, because he screened, or monitored, their performance. Whilst a passenger on one long cross-country flight I was watching the Flight Engineer intensely, intending to learn as much as I could and wondering why he kept looking at me nervously. At the end of the flight the crew were doing their pre-landing checks, and the Flight Engineer seemed hard pressed. When the Pilot called over the intercom "Tail Wheel," the Engineer turned to me and said, "Will you check it?" "What do I check it for?" I asked. "Aren't you a Screen?" he replied. "No," I said, "I'm only here for air experience." He seemed quite relieved as he dashed back to do the check. Obviously a case of mistaken identity.

At Christmas the unit had an unofficial three-day break and on the spur of the moment I decided to visit my cousin Pam who was in digs in Cambridge. She was seventeen years old at the time and realising that as soon as she was eighteen she would be drafted into war work, decided to go back to university. London University had been evacuated to Kings College, Cambridge, and Pam was lodging with the Mascels in Cambridge. Jack Mascel was a Sergeant Navigator, based at RAF Waterbeach, some six or seven miles north of Cambridge where he was able to make frequent visits home to his wife Doris, or 'Queeny' as he used to call her, often accompanied by his crew. The house always seemed to have a party atmosphere. I learned that Pam was spending Christmas with them because she did not have the train fare to Bridgewater, where her Mother was still doing war work. That being so, I decided to inflict myself on them. I was, however, able to make a contribution. On Christmas day when most things were closed and all were at a loss for entertainment, I announced that I knew of a Service Club that was holding a Christmas party in Cambridge. This then was where we all went and spent a very enjoyable day. Regrettably Jack Mansel did not survive the war. He was killed on operations shortly after.

Whilst waiting to join a crew, I would usually manage to arrange my day off on the same day as Paddy Curtis at nearby Stradishall and he usually managed to arrange his on 'market day' at Haverhill. The pubs in Haverhill were open all day on market days and that's where we spent most of our time. This strengthened our friendship and when our

LEARNING TO FLY

next leave was due, we travelled to London together where he introduced me to his stepsister, 'Rene'. She was about ten years older than us, married, with her husband in the Army in Italy. She lived alone in a one bedroom flat near Swiss Cottage, seemed delighted to see us, and persuaded us to stay the night. We bedded down on a mattress on the lounge floor. Paddy also introduced me to his Aunt, whose husband was caretaker of a block of flats in neighbouring St. Johns Wood. His Aunt worked as a barmaid in 'The Duke of York' where we spent the evening and well into the night. The next day we went our separate ways, Paddy to his home in Torquay and I to Aunt Mell's in Bridgewater.

Shortly after our return, I was introduced to a tall, well built, Australian Flight Sergeant Pilot. His name was Cyril Woolnough, and he was the Captain of the crew of which I was to be part. Cyril introduced me to the rest of the crew. "This is Ian Ravenscroft, the bomb aimer." He was a Canadian Flying Officer. "This is Bert Haggerstone, the Navigator." He was a Flight Lieutenant from Yorkshire. "This is Ginger Smith, the Wireless Operator." He was a Scottish Sergeant. "This is Harry Silzer, mid-upper gunner." He was a Canadian Sergeant. "And this is Eric Smith, rear gunner." He was a Sergeant and a Londoner. As a crew we were almost unique in that once we started operational flying, we never ever had a temporary replacement nor did any of the crew ever have to fly with another crew as a temporary replacement.

Except for the two Officers, we all shared the same

accommodation, in a 'Nissan Hut.' A Nissan hut consisted of a large area of corrugated steel sheet in the shape of half a tube with either end filled with a timber wall containing a door and a window. It measured approximately 50ft. long by 20ft. wide by 10ft. high at the apex and was extremely cold in winter. Although we bonded together well, we also tended to form paired friendships. I found myself becoming friendly with Eric Smith, because he had a good sense of humour. One day he said to me, "Let's go out for a drink." "I've hardly got any money," I replied. "That's alright," he said, "We'll take the locals on at darts and when we win they'll buy our drinks" I could be forgiven for thinking that he was an expert darts player so off we went. In a couple of games, both of which we lost, our money ran out and we returned to camp and to bed.

The main object of the Conversion Unit was to accustom the Pilot and the Flight Engineer to work together in handling a large four engined aircraft. The flying training, therefore, consisted of repeated take-offs, circuits and landings, both by night and by day, initially with an instructor, and then solo, sometimes landing at neighbouring airfields. The whole programme was compressed into a fortnight and finished with two 5-hour flights around the UK, one by day and the other at night. We were then ready to get to know the aircraft in which we were to fly on operations, the Lancaster. To this end in early February 1944, the crew headed off to No. 5 L.F.S. (Lancaster Finishing School) at Syerston, between Newark and Nottingham.

6
LANCASTERS

We arrived at Syerston for a three-week stay of intensive flying training much of it similar to that at Wratting Common with the addition of practice bombing on the bombing range at Wainfleet which was situated on the mud flats of the Wash. We also practiced 'fighter affiliation,' both day and night. This consisted of working with a fighter, usually a Hurricane, where the fighter would carry out simulated attacks on the Lancaster which would take quite violent evasive action with the two air gunners simulating defensive fire.

With the busy schedule we didn't have a lot of time for socialising but one evening Eric, Harry and I went out devoid of any plan. The road outside the camp gates went from Nottingham to Newark and we started to hitchhike in both directions. The first car to offer us a lift was going to Nottingham, so that was where we went. As we walked along the city streets we met some girls in party mood and asked them where the nearest dance hall was. "What d'you want to go there for?" one asked. "What else?" we queried. "Come with us," they said. They took us to a lively pub where, partying boisterously, we made some new, but very temporary friends. This was our one and only visit to Nottingham. A few days later we were on our way to our first operational squadron, No. 61 at Coningsby, the station at which Chevy and I had arrived during the ill fated Augsburg raid just after we had left Halton two years before.

The total number of personnel on the base must have increased in the interim for we were now accommodated in a Nissan hut on the other side of the road from the camp gates. It was the end of February and uncomfortably cold in the huts at night once the large stove in the centre had gone out. For the next two weeks we followed the same training routine of 'circuits and bumps,' practice bombing and 'fighter affil' until we felt that we had gelled together as a crew and were performing like a well-oiled machine.

Cyril, our Pilot and 'skipper', was the first to be introduced to operational flying. He had to do his 'second dickey' trip. This was an operational sortie with another crew when he acted as second Pilot or, more exactly, as a passenger to experience an operational sortie. To take our minds off the strain of waiting for his return the rest of the crew enjoyed a night-out in Boston. Lincolnshire, of course.

By then I had become a little disenchanted with my old motorcycle which I had managed to get to Coningsby. The problem with a night out in Boston was that it had to end at about ten o'clock when the last bus left. So on this occasion Eric the Rear Gunner, persuaded me to take him into Boston on the bike and we enjoyed ourselves till after midnight. On the return journey, on a deserted stretch of road, 4 miles out of Boston, the engine of the bike came to a sudden stop and so did we. "It couldn't have happened at a better spot," I said, "there's the canal, let's shove it in." "No! No!" he said, "Look, there's a signal box. Let's ask the signalman to look after it until we can come back and put it on the train." I didn't argue and the signalman agreed to co-operate. Then we took stock. We were eight miles from the base and it was two o'clock in the morning. I said, "Well, we'd better get walking." "Then here," he said, "I've got some Benzedrine Tablets from out of a survival kit. If we take one it'll help us on our way." Having each taken a tablet we set off with renewed vigour. We covered the eight miles in less than two hours. Benzedrine was only supposed to be taken as a last resort, in extreme circumstances, as they were a very powerful stimulant. We realised this the next morning when the effects had worn off and we had difficulty in waking up.

We didn't have long to wait for our first operation as a crew. On the 15th March, 1944, we were briefed to attack Stuttgart in southern Germany. Full of apprehension that our lives were on the line we were pleasantly surprised to find the opposition not as fierce as we had expected. There was one anxious moment, though, when we spotted an enemy fighter. Fortunately, he seemed intent on other prey than us and he soon disappeared.

Ten days later we took part in an attack on Essen, in the Ruhr. This completed the almost total devastation of this city which contained the famous Krupps Works. Four days later the squadron was again assembled in the briefing room for an attack on Nuremberg. We were excluded on this occasion as Cyril, our skipper, had been grounded for a few days suffering from "a bubble in the ear." When we heard the radio news the next day we considered ourselves fortunate to have missed the operation. The bulletin announcing the raid admitted to 180 bombers being lost. This was some four times the usual figure. This figure was later down sized, but never announced, down to 108 bombers, still over double the usual.

This was the last operation carried out by our squadron before a landmark change in bombing policy came into force. The bombing onslaught on Germany was switched to strategic targets in France and the Low Countries in preparation for 'D Day.' A week after Nuremberg we attacked a large aircraft factory in Toulouse, in the south of France, which was reputed to be producing military aircraft for the Germans. The attack was led by Group Captain Leonard Cheshire V.C., who's marking of the target was so accurate that we almost missed it. The red 'spot fire' was burning inside the building having penetrated the roof.

Our own performance failed to match this. We were hit by anti aircraft fire over the target and lost all our hydraulic oil. Then we caught the slipstream of another bomber and the jolt from the turbulence jerked our undercarriage out of its locks. With no hydraulic pressure to hold it in place the undercarriage dropped to a halfway position where it trailed for the whole of the return journey. This increased the drag considerably and therefore, the fuel consumption. This resulted in us having to land short of our Lincolnshire base at RAF Gaydon in Warwickshire. Even though we had lost our hydraulics we were able to lock the undercarriage down and work the flaps by using a compressed air back-up system. Gaydon was not equipped to do major repairs to Lancasters so we decided to return to Coningsby as soon as possible. With enough emergency air pressure left to operate the flaps down, up and down again, we refuelled, took off and flew back to Coningsby with our undercarriage fixed firmly down all the way.

Shortly after this, with little or no warning, we were told to pack our kit as we were about to move to a different base. Coningsby was to become a 'Pathfinder' station and we were to move to Skellingthorpe, about three miles South West of Lincoln. This was a relatively easy move because all we did was to throw our 'kit bags' into our Lancaster, fly across to Skellingthorpe, and get ourselves a billet. Though we didn't know it at the time, this was the birth of "The Independent Air Force" as 5 Group was to become known. The intention was for 5 Group, with a strength of about 250 Lancasters, to concentrate on diversionary targets and so split the enemy defences.

In the next two weeks we did four uneventful sorties, two to rail junctions in the Paris area, one to an ammunition dump in a French wooded area and one to the German border town of Aachen. Then, for reasons unknown to us, we were suddenly switched back to attacking major German cities. Within the space of a week three received our attention, Brunswick, Schweinfurt and Munich.

In Munich we received a hot reception. We were over the city and focused on the target indicator. The Bomb-Aimer's voice could be heard over the intercom. "Left-left, steady, steady, right, steady," when suddenly we were engulfed in a flood of brilliant light. Just about every searchlight in Munich was pointing a finger of light at us. This usually meant that an enemy fighter was homing in on us. In spite of this, Ian, the Bomb-Aimer, insisted that Cyril keep flying straight and level until we had dropped our bombs. "Bombs gone, bomb-doors closed." We all breathed a sigh of relief and Cyril and I went into 'our act.' The standard method of attempting to evade a fighter was to 'corkscrew,' that is to make the aircraft describe a spiral path through the air by diving, rolling and climbing. Cyril and I had practiced a technique for exaggerating this. He was powerfully built and with his strength, could force the aircraft into the tightest turns, dives and climbs whilst I would operate the throttles (the nearest equivalent to a car accelerator) in such a way as to exaggerate the movements even further. Thus, not only did we manage to evade the fighter but also, after about five or six minutes, we found ourselves in the relative comfort of darkness.

However, this was not the end of our troubles. Heading back to base we ran into some severe icing conditions. The leading edge of a Lancaster wing consisted of a porous material through which de-icing fluid could be made to seep. Unfortunately, on this occasion conditions were so bad that the arrangement did not prevent ice from building up on the wings. The build-up of ice worked to our detriment in three different ways. First it altered the aerofoil shape of the wing and so reduced lift. Then it added considerably to the overall weight of the aircraft and finally, it built up in the engine air intakes and reduced the power of the engines. It was possible to direct the warm air flowing through the engine radiators into the carburettor to eliminate the ice, but warm air is less dense than cold air and so it still resulted in loss of power.

With the build up of ice we steadily lost height until we finally broke cloud at about 1500 ft. Here the ambient air was warmer and we started to lose the ice. We also found ourselves at low level over another unidentified German town that was being attacked by another force of Bomber Command. The view was as spectacular as the danger was great, and we lost no time in getting clear of the inferno.

Even then our troubles were not at an end. Having lost the ice we started to climb. Just as we were approaching our intended altitude the port inner engine suddenly started to flash with small tongues of flame shooting in all directions and the propeller speed fluctuating wildly. It was obvious that the engine was about to burst into flames and so, even before Cyril had time to give the order, with three deft movements I cut off the fuel supply and feathered the engine. The feathering button switched the appropriate mechanism to cause the pitch of the propeller to coarsen to the extent that the blades faced into the oncoming airflow at an angle that would prevent them from 'wind-milling.' So we continued with three engines generating extra power and consuming more fuel overall than four good engines

A rough calculation showed me that by the time we reached England we would be dangerously short of fuel and so Cyril our Captain, Bert the Navigator, and Ginger the Wireless Operator, started making arrangements for an emergency landing. We were directed to land at RAF Tangmere, on the South coast, a fighter airfield that had figured largely in the Battle of Britain four years before. Dawn was breaking when we landed and while we went off to have some much needed refreshment, a small team of mechanics examined the offending engine to determine the cause of the failure. On our return to the plane we were greeted with the news that an inclined drive shaft had sheered. This meant an engine change and after a brief exchange of signals, a Lancaster was despatched from Skellingthorpe to return us to our base.

When we moved from Coningsby I had left my motorcycle at Coningsby station where it lay, after having been shipped by rail from the signal box on the way back from Boston. Now Ian Ravenscroft, our Bomb-Aimer, asked me if he could buy it. I said, "You can have it for nothing if you get it over from Coningsby." About a week later he came to me and said, "I've changed my mind about the motorcycle. I don't think I want it." "Where is it now?" I asked. "In Lincoln station parcels office," he replied. "Well," I concluded, "It can stay there, it's not doing any harm." I was glad to see the back of it, for, though it had served me well in its early days, lack of maintenance, due to lack of time gradually turned it into a liability.

We now resumed operations against military targets in the occupied countries. At the end of April we set out to attack an ordinance factory at Bordeaux but, as there was some difficulty in locating the target, and accuracy was vital over France, the operation was aborted and we returned with our bombs.

A fortnight later we were briefed to attack a rail junction at Lile, in Belgium. As we crossed the Belgian coast we ran into some heavy Flak which damaged the coolant system of the starboard inner engine. This caused the engine to rapidly over-heat and burst into flames. Again our high-speed 'feathering' action had the engine stopped in a few seconds and with my finger on the fire extinguisher button, I was relieved to see the flames die down whilst I still had 'another card to play.' We completed the attack and returned to base on three engines. The next morning we were not surprised to see that the aircraft was full of holes. We were a little surprised that none of the crew were.

That evening, we were again assembled in the briefing room for our next operation. This was a German military camp at Bourgleapold, in Holland. Before the briefing started, the CO announced that we were required to supply a crew for the Pathfinder Force, PFF or 8 Group as it was called. It consisted of an elite force of six squadrons based in Huntingdonshire. Their task was to precede the attack, locate the target, and mark it with special pyrotechnics for the main force of bombers to aim at. He asked for a volunteer crew but was greeted with stony silence. "In that case," he said, "we'll have to draw lots." He put a number of pieces of paper in a hat and went round the Captains, who took one each. He then gathered them in and studied them for a minute. "I'll tell you who the lucky winner is on your return," he said. "Tell us now, tell us now," was the cry. To stop the general clamour, he announced the 'lucky winner' and all but one crew breathed a sigh of relief.

Later that night we took off and headed for Holland. There was some difficulty in locating the target and as accuracy was of the essence in the occupied countries, we were instructed to abort the operation and return to base. I calculated that we would be 3500 lbs. over our maximum landing weight on our return and a general discussion took place over the intercom as to whether we should get rid of three 1000 lb. and one 500 lb. bombs, or whether we should lose the one 4000 lb. "Cookie," as it was called. The matter was soon settled when Cyril told me to make the decision and I opted for the 'Cookie' to give us a margin of error. This was dropped in the middle of the North Sea and we proceeded to base.

Unknown to us, while battling through the defences, our compressed air wheel brake system had been damaged, and this we did not discover until we were hurtling down the runway on landing and found that we had no effective brakes. We sped past the end of the runway, across a road, and into a field until we hit a broad, deep ditch which buckled the undercarriage and brought the plane to an abrupt halt on its belly. The 4000 lb. bombs had thin casings and were prone to explode on impact, whether fused or not. Had we retained the 'Cookie', it is more than likely we would have been blown to pieces. The entry in my Logbook stated "Returned with Bombs, Crashed on Landing". Although understated, we laughingly referred to our Logbooks as 'The Greatest Unpublished Thriller of the War'.

The next morning we were summoned to the briefing room, where the CO announced, with regret, that the crew that had been earmarked for 'Pathfinders,' had failed to return from the previous night's operation. He, therefore, proposed to draw lots again and this time the unlucky crew would go straight to the Pathfinder training base that day. This time it was our crew that drew the short straw and we were on our way within hours.

After three weeks at the training base at RAF Warboys we took our place on a Pathfinder squadron. To our delight this turned out to be 97 Squadron, at Coningsby, one of the two squadrons that had displaced us to Skellingthorpe. Our days at Coningsby didn't start well for Eric Smith and me. When we were at Coningsby with 61 squadron we were billeted in Nissan huts in the over-flow site. We had discovered too late that the billeting arrangements were haphazard and we could have just occupied an empty room in the Sergeant's Mess block with its luxurious central heating. Anxious not to repeat this mistake, we found and occupied an empty room in the mess. Unfortunately for us the billeting arrangements with the new incumbents was much better organised and we soon had a visit from the Warrant Officer Discip instructing us to decamp. He returned the next day to find us still there. We claimed that we had received inoculations, which made our arm stiff, and were therefore excused heavy duties for forty-eight hours. Moving our kit was heavy duty. Warrant Officer Wells decided not to argue with us but to put us on his 'black list.' He gave us forty-eight hours to get out with which we complied. This little incident had disastrous results for me in the months to come. Results which effected my whole career.

The other mistake I made was to write to Chevy, in Ireland, to say that I was now on the same squadron, at the same camp as we had been on together when we first left Halton. Although I had pointedly omitted to name the squadron or the station the censor had taken exception and despatched the offending letter to my Commanding Officer with a recommendation that I be charged with breaching the 'official secrets act.' The CO seemed to think that the censor had gone over the top a bit, but he had no option but to charge me, though he only sentenced me to a 'reprimand.'

When we first arrived on the station, and booked in, we were given the job of taking a dead body from the morgue in the sick quarters, to the railway station. We did not know for sure how the young man had died but we understood that he was, in fact, a war casualty and his body was being sent to his home for burial. We were all a little taken aback when, on arriving at the sick quarters, Harry Silzer, our Canadian mid-upper gunner, asked in a loud voice, "Where's the stiff?" This was the measure of the brutalising effect that the war was having on us.

For the next two weeks we continued the flying training that we had been taught at the Pathfinder Training School. Then we were summoned to the briefing room. The big wall map showed the target as a point on the Normandy coast. "The target is St. Pierre Du Monde, a large German coastal battery," the CO announced. "And the target is not for tonight but for the morning, five o'clock. This is the invasion that we've all been waiting for," he added. (later known as D-Day). "You can all go to bed now and get some sleep. You'll be called at three."

This was to be a world changing event that was widely expected, but nobody knew when, and it remained to be one of the best kept secrets of the war. I lay on my bed tingling with excitement at the thought of the task at hand and knowing what the whole world was waiting to hear.

It was still dark when we excitedly donned our flying kit and boarded the shuttle buses to our aircrafts. Our Maintenance Crew, who where never aware of our targets, may have sensed the apprehension in the air that morning. As we taxied into position and began to open the throttle, the Ground Staff that stood at the end of the runway began to wave as they wished us the ritual 'Bon Voyage'.

Dawn was breaking as we took off and soon the sky was filled with Lancasters. A little over an hour later we were over our target. The broken cloud allowed us to run up on our 'aiming-point' but denied us the panoramic view of the vast armada of ships below. After annihilating the objective coastal gun installation, we turned for base and soon began to feel vulnerable at the lack of fighter escort in broad daylight, but encountered no opposition and returned safely. Later in the day however, we heard that our CO had failed to return from the operation and one of the crews claimed to have seen him shot down by an enemy fighter. That same night as the invasion continued, we were out again attacking another German military installation further inland.

When we heard a radio news bulletin stating that we had established a firm foothold on the Normandy bridgehead, the British and American Armies in Italy had entered Rome, and the Germans were in retreat all along the Russian front. "This," we thought, "must be the beginning of the end."

Having survived these operations without loss, we were now owed another leave. Operational aircrew enjoyed certain privileges, we slept between sheets, were allowed to wear shoes rather than boots, and were given twice as much leave, seven days every six weeks. For this leave we planned to drive to London in an old car Eric had bought himself. But first it had to be taxed, so we drove it to Lincoln, got our Tax Disc from the council offices, and were half way back when we had a puncture. We really needed new tyres but nothing was available that did not directly benefit the war effort. We were busy stuffing grass into the outer tube when a couple of young teen-aged boys stopped to watch us. We had an idea. We asked them if they had a cycle puncture outfit, which they did and which they sold to us at an exorbitant price. We managed to patch the tyre up, inflated it with their cycle pump, and limped back to camp too late to go anywhere. The next morning we went to London by train.

In London, I telephoned Paddy's sister, Rene, who seemed delighted to hear from me and invited me to stay on her lounge floor, as was typical of her hospitality for her brothers or their military friends. Eager for our news she opened with, "Anything exciting happened?" "Not much," I responded, nonchalantly. "Weren't you on the invasion?" she asked. "Oh yes," I said, "but that wasn't very eventful." Compared with the last time that I had seen her, which was shortly after the two operations where we had lost an engine in one, and crashed on the other, the D-Day sorties turned out to be safe trips. The success of D-Day had clearly excited the nation.

The next morning Rene went to work, leaving me to cook my own breakfast. She phoned me from her west-end office to ask how I was managing. "Well, I've burned the bacon," I said, "So I think I'll boil the egg." This was my first attempt at cooking and since each item represented a week's ration, I desisted from all further culinary experiments. From there I went on to Paddy's mother's house in Torquay. She seemed to have adopted me as another son and when I heard Paddy's cousin, Betty, who was in the WRNS, call her 'Aunty Lena,' I did the same which seemed to please her.

Back at Coningsby, we started to adjust to the differences in the Pathfinder aircraft. They were all fitted with 'H2S' the latest radar device that the Germans were unable to jam. H2S would scan the ground below the plane and produce, on a cathode ray tube, the outline of towns from which the Bomb-Aimer could identify the target area and drop flares or reference markers. This screen was located at the Navigator's table and the Navigator's seat was replaced with a bench to share with the Bomb-Aimer. Because the Flight Engineer stood between the Bomb-Aimer, in his new location, and the bombsight, in the nose of the plane, it was thought a good idea to get the Flight Engineer to do the bombing whenever the traditional bombsite was to be used. Surprisingly, on the bombing range, the Flight Engineer's results were, on average, better than their Bomb-Aimer's. The briefing arrangements, however, did not change and the Flight Engineers were usually uninformed about target details. Whilst targeting the Normandy town of Caen, I was doing the bombing and in the flash of the bombs I was able to see water. "Oh shit," I said, "the bombs have gone into water." "That's good," Cyril replied, "we're hitting the bridges"

Cyril and I often used to browse in the Intelligence Library and one day we came across a report advising that German anti-aircraft gunners were instructed, on firing their second salvo, to allow for the target aircraft to make a dive to port in an attempt to evade the shells. We therefore resolved to do the opposite and from then on, during training flights, we drilled ourselves to climb to starboard. We found that when we put this into practice on operations, we quickly distanced ourselves from the potentially lethal shellfire as it flashed away in the opposite direction.

Cyril, as a Flight Sergeant, was the only non-commissioned Pilot on the squadron. We all felt that, because he did not hob-nob with the Flight Commanders and the CO, we may be getting some of the less pleasant tasks. We suggested to him that he should apply for a commission. "I don't want to be an Officer," he growled in his Australian accent. When we explained to him that we all wanted him to have a commission and that it was as much for our benefit as his, he agreed. His application was accepted immediately. His report described him as 'A rough-cut Diamond.'

Towards the end of June, we started practicing formation flying. A rumour went round that it was planned to mount a two thousand-bomber raid on Berlin in conjunction with the American eighth air force. The Lancaster was designed as a night bomber and was not sufficiently stable in flight for tight formations. Ultimately, the inevitable happened. Two Lancasters from Coningsby collided in mid air. Of the combined crew of fourteen, there was only one survivor, who managed to bail out by parachute and almost landed on the burning wreckage of the two planes. He was immediately put into another Lancaster as a passenger before he lost his nerve. But alas, it was too late. Before they could take off he went berserk and had to be let out. As a result he was classified L.M.F. (Lack of Moral Fibre), stripped of his brevy (the half wing that all aircrew wore on the left of their chest) and reduced to the ranks. He left the station in disgrace.

We were continuously reminded of the importance of security. It was most important that we carried with us on operations nothing that in the event of capture would give the Germans any indication of our unit or the location of our base such as bus or cinema ticket stubs. To reinforce the message a type of poster was displayed on the briefing room wall featuring a forlorn individual with his empty trouser pockets turned inside out, staring wistfully at a French Brothel. Above it, in bold letters, was the following message. "N'oubliez pas de vider vos poches avant de partir en operation." There was no translation. Needless to say curiosity ensured that everyone found out that it translated, "Do not forget to empty your pockets before leaving on operations." It was such a powerful message that sixty years later, though I am not a French speaker, I remember the French, verbatim.

The authorities provided us with some little items to help us in all eventualities. Should we successfully parachute to safety on land and evade immediate capture, our flying boots were designed as shoes with leggings. At the point where the two joined was a narrow band of uninsulated fabric and let into a little pocket in one legging, was a knife to cut off the leggings, leaving us with a good pair of walking shoes.

The top two buttons of our blue battle dress, when cut off and placed one on top of the other, would form a compass. Hanging from our collars at all times was a referee's type whistle to maintain contact with each other in the even of a ditching in the sea. No ties or other restrictions were allowed to be worn around the neck as these may shrink and choke us if immersed in water. Finally, to ensure that our dead bodies could be easily identified, we wore, dangling on a piece of string around our necks, identity disks of a fiberous material with our name and number on them. In addition we wore our name and number on a leather strip sewn onto our battle dress tops just above the right breast pocket.

In addition to all this we were offered the option of carrying a hand gun. We each drew from the armoury a Colt .38 revolver and went to the pistol range to try them out. My own experience was that with six rounds, fired at a distance of 30m I did not hit the target once. When I considered its possible use as a means to avoid capture, I thought of those famous words from the Bible, "He that lives by the sword shall die by the sword." Consequently, I put it away in my locker until I returned it on completion of our operational tour. The rest of the crew did the same, except Harry Silzer, our Canadian Mid-upper Gunner. We all thought he saw himself as a wild-west gun slinger. Whenever operations were on for that night he would strut around with his gun stuck in his belt and invariably took it with him on operations.

During a single week in the middle of August we carried out six operational sorties, two at night and four by daylight. One of the daylight raids was an attack on the submarine pens at Bordeaux. We had no fighter escort but we encountered no enemy fighters. The Flak was not intense but it was accurate enough for us to hear the shrapnel splattering on the exposed bombs in the bomb bay beneath our feet, and to smell the Cordite as it was drawn into the air intake. As we crossed the French coast on our return shortly after, we saw a couple of warships a few miles off the coast. At the same time we heard a voice over the R-T, "I have a hang-up, shall I drop it on those ships or are they ours?" When a bomb failed to release electrically, it was referred to as a 'Hang-up' and had to be released manually by mechanism that was accessible through small hatches in the floor above the bomb bay. The reply from the Master Bomber was curt and immediate, "Negative!"

Another daylight raid was on Deelan, a German fighter station in Holland. The squadron were in loose formation and intent on the target. So much so that one of the aircraft failed to notice another Lancaster directly below it. The plane below kept pace with the forward trajectory of the bombs from the one above and was eventually hit by them, disintegrating with all its occupants in a large cloud of fire and smoke. This explosion managed to damage the plane above, putting two of its engines out of action and causing it to gradually lose height until eventually it ditched in the sea some five miles off the Dutch coast. The German E boats (motor torpedo boats) immediately put to sea to capture the crew but the American 'Thunderbolt' fighters, that were escorting us, swooped down and attacked them, driving them back to port. Some time later a specially adapted Wellington bomber arrived carrying an airborne lifeboat which was dropped, by parachute, to them. Later still, they were met halfway home by a Royal Navy destroyer and brought to safety. As a 'reward' the Pilot was made 'station Survival and Rescue Officer.'

LANCASTERS

In the middle of August we were briefed for a 'Gardening Operation.' Gardening was the code name for the planting of mines in the sea. The target was the Swinemunde Canal, near Stettin and our function, as second flare wave, was to provide back-up illumination of the target area. There had been the usual directions from S/Ldr. Porter, the Master Bomber. As we aligned ourselves for our bombing run, there was a brief silence. Suddenly we heard the same voice say, "I've bought it boys I'm bailing out." I pondered these words for a few minutes thinking, "How can he 'bail out'? They must be right down on the water." Finally it dawned on me this was just a euphemism. He surely must known they couldn't survive.

By the end of August the Russians were closing in on East Prussia (now part of Poland). It was decided to mount an attack on Koningsburg, the capital, to impress the Russians with the strength of our aerial clout. Koningsburg was too far for the Mosquito aircraft to do the final visual marking and so two Lancasters, one of which was ours, were earmarked for the job. To maintain an element of surprise it was necessary for us to remain below the reach of the German radar for as long as possible. Our route took us over southern Sweden where, because the Germans were in Denmark, across the Skagerak and the Kattegat, we had to fly so low that we could see people walking about in the brightly lit streets. The Swedes fired off a few anti- aircraft rounds, as was expected of them, but nowhere near us.

Some 50 miles before the target, we climbed to our operational height of 10,000 ft. The main force of bombers was to come in at 15,000 ft. and between the two heights was a thin layer of cloud. Between the two, also, lay the maximum effective height of the light Flak. Consequently, the two pathfinder Lancasters bore the brunt of the entire anti-aircraft defences of the city. In addition to the heavy shells bursting around us we could see the lighter tracer shells being hose-piped at us. As soon as we crossed the coast, we had to take violent evasive action and we were grateful for Cyril's strength and his ability to 'throw the Lancaster about.' Nevertheless it was necessary for us to work our way out to sea again and prepare for another attempt. Meanwhile the other pathfinder Lancaster had succumbed to the heavy defences and had hit the ground clear of the city where its target indicator exploded and was burning brightly. Because of the delay, the main force of bombers was now approaching and seeing the target indicator through the thin layer of cloud, aimed their bombs at it, resulting in the devastation of some open fields.

When the P.R.U. (Post-operational Reconnaissance Unit) photographs were received, and the results known, a repeat operation was arranged for three days later. This time, with improved tactics and weather conditions, the attack was very successful and the authorities well pleased. This was our thirtieth sortie and marked the end of our first tour of operations. Normally the crew would have dispersed to various training locations for about six months before returning in freshly formed crews for a second tour of twenty sorties. However, Air Vice Marshal Bennett, AOC Pathfinder Group, in order to keep his highly trained and specialised crews for as long as possible, offered them a deal. If they undertook to continue with their second tour as a follow on they could have a five-sortie discount. In other words their total requirement would be for forty-five sorties, after which they could not be called upon to do any more. This was an offer we could not refuse. Nevertheless we were still sent off on two weeks 'end of tour' leave.

As usual, I headed for London and 'The Duke of York' in St. John's Wood, where Paddy's Aunt worked as an evening bar maid. Her husband was caretaker of a large block of luxury flats in St. John's Wood, one of which they occupied and which gave them a very exclusive address. I was invariably invited to spend a night or two with them. Each time I visited the pub, at the start of every leave, I would go into the public bar for a chat with 'Bill'. Bill was a true cockney with a fantastic sense of humour. I would sit and listen to him tell a string of new jokes while his wife and brother-in-law, who were always with him, would act as his laughing audience, even though they had heard them all before. On returning to the saloon bar on this occasion I was introduced to a short, plump, rather jolly lady in her forties, who was the personal dresser to Evelyn Leigh, the famous star of stage and screen. In the true tradition of the theatre the jolly little lady was erratic and totally unpredictable. After closing time when only the privileged guests remained, she was standing at one end of the bar while I was at the other. Suddenly, without any warning, she started running towards me and with a shout of "Catch me!" she leapt into the air. Needless to say we both ended up in a heap on the floor.

We enjoyed each other's company and as she was also a guest at the flat, she kept persuading me to stay another day. I was due to visit Aunt Mel and Pam, at Burnham-on-sea, in Somerset and it was necessary for me to send a series of telegrams rescheduling my visit. Four days and three telegrams later, I finally boarded the train at Paddington somewhat the worse for all the drink that I had consumed.

Aunt Mel and Pam were working in a shadow munitions factory and were accommodated in an apartment within a single storey timber complex. They had managed to find a bed for me and I spent the next two days 'drying out.' Pam came to the station to see me off on the early morning train to Torquay. Whilst waiting for the train I was telling her all about our trip across France on our way to Halton. She could hardly get her breath for laughing.

I arrived in Torquay to find that Rene had relocated to her mother's house to support her in her ordeal. Her mother had received a telegram from the Air Ministry to say that Paddy was missing on operations. They did not know whether he was alive or dead. On leave, at the same time, was Paddy's brother, Des. Des was an Officer Navigator on Coastal Command Mosquitoes mostly employed in attacking coastal shipping. He had the same carefree attitude as Paddy and we got on well together. He, his sister Rene, and I would go out as a trio most nights enjoying ourselves into the early hours of the morning.

I returned to London a day before my leave expired in order

to pay a long overdue visit to Mrs. Miles in Twickenham. At this time the V1s or flying bombs, or 'Doodlebugs' as they were often called, were bombarding London. They were quite nerve-wracking as one could clearly hear the engine as they flew overhead. Suddenly the engine would cut out. People would hold their breath and wait. About ten seconds later there was an almighty bang. Those who were not involved in the explosion would then carry-on whatever they were doing before. That night, as I was going to bed in the spare bedroom, I put out the light and drew the blackout curtains. Then I looked at the window and thought, "If the window's blown in I could be cut to ribbons by flying glass." So I closed the curtains again. In the middle of the night there was a deafening 'bang' which woke every one in an instant. I found that the window had indeed been blown in but the curtains had held back the flying glass. A blast can do strange things. We found that the front door of the flat, which was partially glazed, and firmly locked with a Yale type lock, was now swinging open but otherwise intact.

By now, the war in Western Europe was going well. The allies had advanced in a big ark liberating Paris and heading for the Rhine which was the German border. We were now able to return to attacking targets in Germany. On one of these sorties we had run into the usual anti-aircraft shellfire over the target when a shell burst rather too close to us and pieces of shrapnel penetrated the windscreen. One piece hit Cyril in the chest but the generous padding of his 'Mae West,' as our life jackets were called, protected him from harm. Another piece buried itself in the structure of the aircraft where I had been standing a moment before. Luckily I had just bent down to despatch a bundle of 'window' through the chute. Window was the code name for the strips of tinsel that we released from time to time. They had the effect of filling the German radar screens with white specks making it difficult for them to locate their targets. I thought afterwards, had I not bent down at that moment, I would have received the shrapnel in my unprotected side.

On another occasion, we were flying quietly over an undefended area of Germany when we were suddenly struck by lightning. There was a blinding flash and an almighty bang and for about five minutes we could see nothing. When our normal vision returned everything was just as it had been before. Every part of an aircraft is electrically bonded to the next and the plane acted as a conductor for the lightning.

We were usually routed over known undefended areas of Germany and sometimes this gave us long periods of quiet, uneventful flight. On one such occasion I began to feel drowsy so I sat on my parachute on the floor to fill in the log that I had to keep. I was trying to decide whether we were doing plus or minus 155 knots when the engines cut. In a flash I changed from the auxiliary to the main petrol tanks and the engines burst into life again. I was about to say something when I was interrupted. "How's that, Eric?" I heard Cyril say on the intercom "That's better, Skip, no more contrails," replied Eric, the rear gunner. That made me stop and think. I had dozed off and missed the previous conversation when apparently Eric had reported that we were making contrails which could lead enemy fighters to us. Pulling the throttles back fast and then opening up again could break these. It was the cutting of the engines that had restored me to consciousness. I quietly returned the tanks to 'auxiliary' and said nothing.

On a warm summer's day in August it was decided to hold a swimming gala for the base. The venue was the open-air pool at Woodall Spa. RAF Woodall was a satellite to Coningsby and housed our pathfinder Mosquitoes and also the Lancasters of 617 squadron, the 'dam busting' squadron, which were specially modified to carry Barnes Wallace's 12,000 lb. bombs with which they later sank the German battleship, 'Tirpitz,' in a Norwegian fjord. The star of the swimming gala was Coningsby's station commander, Group Captain Evans Evans. The Group Captain was about 6ft. tall, weighed about 400 lbs. with a waist measurement of about 54 in. It was rumoured that he had a twin brother and whenever they met they had to stand side on to shake hands. It was sometimes difficult to tell fact from fiction not that it really mattered so long as it was funny. I was in a small cubicle getting changed when the Group Captain suddenly burst in with, "Room for another, isn't there lad?" The next moment I was shot out of the cubicle like a pea being shelled and obliged to complete my changing in the open.

The event of the day was the plunging, the only event the Group Captain entered for. As soon as he dived in there was a mini tidal wave and all the spectators got splashed. Everybody took it in good humour except Wing Commander

Guy Gibson who was seated in the position of honour by the bath side. He disdainfully flicked the offending drops off his uniform with the back of his hand and with obvious displeasure. Gibson had the use of an office in station headquarters to write his book, "Enemy Coast Ahead," his account of the Dam-buster raid. Later, when the book was finished, he returned to flying and because of his celebrity status, was given an American 'Lightning' long range fighter in which to perform the function of 'Master Bomber' The master bomber's responsibility was to visually check and approve the accuracy of the target marking. He gave us the impression that he thought he was immortal. Fate decreed otherwise. He eventually failed to return from a sortie and was finally confirmed dead.

Group Captain Evans Evans also had an unfortunate career. With little experience of Lancasters he would get involved in flying as often as his duties would allow. One day he decided to take our crew on a practice bombing exercise on the bombing range at Wainfleet. On entering the aircraft, he had difficulty in traversing the main spa which was like a 3ft. high wall across the fuselage. "Give us a shove, Engineer," he said to me. I put my shoulder against his enormous arse and pushed as hard as I could, shooting him forward into the empty area ahead. When we reached our operating altitude the Wireless Operator obtained a wind speed and direction for that height and this was fed into the bombsite computer. An experienced Lancaster Pilot would have told the Flight Engineer what height and air speed he wanted to maintain and the Engineer would have set the necessary power. Evans

Evans decided to do it all himself with the result that we ended the exercise 2,000 ft. higher than we started and with a different wind speed and direction. When I reported this to the bombing leader on our return he said, "God! He'll have an enormous error, we'd better lose the report." Some months later, after we had left the squadron, we heard that he had taken a crew on an operation from which they had failed to return.

On the 23rd. November, 1944, Eric and I went into Boston for a night out. We stayed overnight at the Coronation Club. This was a large boarding house owned and run by a couple whose son had been killed on our squadron. The husband was disabled, having been gassed in World War I. Most of the work was done by the wife whom we always called "Mrs. Woman." She managed to crowd as many as six beds into a single normal sized bedroom and had never been known to turn any of 'her boys' away. I slept soundly, and had the most realistic dream of my life. The dream started with me being helped to my feet in a field by a small group of young men one of who was Paddy. "How did you get back?" I asked him. "I'm not back," he replied, "You're here," meaning Germany. They took me to a house in a town which was obviously German from the shape of the cars in the street. We went down into a cellar where, on the wall, was a large map of the Frankfurt area of Germany. "That's where we are," they said. "But now we're going to get some sleep." I lay in bed for a long time, wondering how I had managed to get back to England. Eventually it dawned on me that the whole thing had been a dream.

The inexplicable thing about this dream was that I had said to my comrades in the cellar, "I must have been shot down by a fighter with upward firing guns." When awake, I dismissed this as a dream-like fantasy as no such thing had ever been heard of. However, unknown to anybody, the Germans were operating their 'Schrage Music' (Slanting Music), as they called it. These were fighters with two 20mm Cannons pointing upwards and sloping slightly forward. They had the advantage of attacking the bombers from their blind underbellies. This weapon was so lethal that few crews that had fallen victim to it had returned to report it. The few that had survived knew not from whence the attack had come. The existence of these fighters only came to light after the war.

The next morning was my twenty first birthday and on returning to camp we were greeted with, "Ops on tonight." We went to the briefing room that evening and there, on the wall, was a large map of southern Germany with a route marked across the Frankfurt area to a town called Breslau, in Upper Silesia. Once again, Breslau was out of range of the Mosquito aircraft and we, and another crew, were to be given the job of visual marking. This time we were to go in at 3000 ft. with guns blazing. "Do you get the feeling they're trying to get rid of us?" I asked in general. We had just finished our pre-op meal of bacon and eggs, a rare treat in wartime, when the news came. "Ops scrubbed." Apparently there was insufficient cloud cover along the route for safety. There was a loud cheer as we prepared to go out and celebrate. We all went down to the 'mucky duck,' as the Black Swan pub, in the village, was called. There we celebrated my twenty first birthday in fine style. Coincidentally, that same day, Paddy's mother heard that he was alive and well and a prisoner of war.

By now we had done thirty-eight operations and I thought it was a good time to make a career move. I applied for a commission. My application would have to be backed by three character references, The Flight Commander, the Engineer Leader and the Warrant Officer Discip. Ever since we first arrived on the station Warrant Officer Wells had been nursing a grudge against Eric and me over the business of the room in the mess. Here was his opportunity. Wells was a tall, well built, 'macho' man and he was more than a little friendly with the Engineer Leader, Flight Lieutenant Roberts, a small, slightly built, rather effeminate sort of man. They shared a car and went on leave together. Within the squadron, they were laughingly referred to as Mr. and Mrs. Wells. I was summoned to the CO's office for a preliminary interview where, on the desk in front of him, were three reports. He started, "The fact that you are an ex Halton apprentice prejudices me in your favour but I can't possibly recommend you with these references." He then proceeded to read me the Warrant Officer's Report. It did not have a good word to say about me and ended, "He is not considered fit to be an NCO (Non-Commissioned Officer) let alone an Officer." The Engineer Leader's report took the same line. The CO, knowing of their relationship, was shrewd enough to guess that I was being victimised. He said, "You've nearly finished your tour you'll soon be posted as an instructor. Why don't you apply again when you get there?" Unfortunately things did not work out like that and another opportunity never came.

A week before Christmas, we set off for an attack on Munich. We were carrying the latest H2S technology on test, with instructions to blind-bomb an airfield outside the city. We had just crossed the French coast when this piece of Radar hardwear ceased to function. Mindful that there was a Christmas party on the camp that night, we persuaded Cyril to return to base on the grounds that we could not carry out our prime purpose. Cyril always did have an acquiescent disposition which, on this occasion, earned him a good telling off from the CO We should have gone on and bombed the city visually. Nevertheless we all enjoyed the Christmas party.

The weather was rather foggy at this time and on our return from an attack on the German cruisers, 'Emden' and 'Koln' in Oslo fjord, we were obliged to land at RAF Milltown which was equipped with F.I.D.O. (Fog Intensive Dispersal Operation) This equipment consisted of two 4 in. diameter pipes, one on each side of the runway along its entire length. The pipes were fitted with burners every few feet and filled with oil. To disperse the fog the oil was ignited and this produced two walls of flame about 10 ft. high, one on either side of the runway. Just as we were touching down there was a blood curdling scream from Eric in the rear turret. "What's the matter?" asked Cyril, in alarm. "I'd been dozing," replied Eric, "and thought I'd gone to hell." The sight was certainly awesome.

LANCASTERS

A week later, on our return from attacking an oil refinery in Poland, we were diverted to RAF Wick, near John O'Groats, in the extreme north of Scotland. The town of Wick was a dry town, that is no alcohol. Three squadrons descended on them and some four hundred thirsty young men drank the Sergeant's and Officer's Messes dry within an hour.

The next day we headed back to base which involved a three-hour flight over the sea. Cyril handed over the controls to me and went down into the nose of the aircraft for a sleep. I enjoyed having control and I also enjoyed the thrill of speed at low level, so I gradually let the aircraft down until it was hurtling over the waves. After a while the Navigator's voice came over the intercom. "What height are you at?" This woke Cyril with a start. "Get up," he said. "We've been like this for ages," I replied. "Well don't go any lower," Cyril concluded and went back to sleep again. The Flight Engineer was considered to be the second Pilot on the Lancaster and on training flights we would often take over the controls and practice landing on clouds. When we got back to Coningsby the fog was closing in again but, just in time, we managed to land at nearby Strubby and were bused back to base on Christmas Eve.

It was during this period of fog that the Germans launched their initially successful Ardennes offensive. This was a sudden, surprise assault, aimed at splitting the allied armies and securing the city of Antwerp. The fog kept all the aircraft on the ground and prevented the allies from responding in their most effective way. When the fog finally lifted and the planes could fly again, they made short work of the advancing German panzers.

Immediately after Christmas and with only one more operation to complete our second tour, we went off on seven days leave. After the usual night in St. Johns Wood, I went on down to Torquay. This time there was only Rene for company and we went everywhere together. In spite of the age difference there was a strong physical attraction, that was mutual and eventually the predictable occurred. A clandestine liaison was formed. On my return to camp Rene accompanied me back to London where she intended to reopen her flat. Before I caught my train she introduced me to a friend who was in the A.T.S. This girl was going up north on the same train as me and so we travelled together. She did not suspect that there was anything between Rene and myself, and she started to try and make arrangements for us to meet in London on her return.

A couple of days after we all got back to camp we did our forty-fifth and last operation to our favourite German city, Munich. This was our fourth visit and as usual we flew over the mountains of Switzerland to hide from the German radar. The Swiss, like the Swedes, fired token Flak, but nowhere near us. On the return leg to base we threw caution to the wind and set maximum cruising power on the engines. We reached base shortly after the Mosquitoes and well ahead of all the other Lancasters. Symbolic sighs of relief turned to elation upon landing as we reflected on the odds of surviving the maximum two complete tour of operations, especially when thoughts then turned to the number of lost comrades.

The next day we all went on two weeks 'end of tour' leave proud to be able to permanently wear our 'Pathfinder Badge.' This was a small brass eagle worn at the top of the left hand breast pocket of our tunics. It signified the successful completion of our tours with the Pathfinder Force. Before going our separate ways however we decided to have a last fling in Boston where we booked our beds for the night at Mrs. Woman's Coronation club.

We enjoyed a great evening in spite of the snow that had started to fall. After a good night's sleep in a crowded bedroom I came down to breakfast. I had a train to catch. In front of me, on the table, was a sealed envelope with my name on it. Also on it was a note saying, "Not to be opened till you are on the train." It was from Mrs. Woman's daughter and although I was consumed with curiosity, I did as instructed and put the letter in my pocket.

After saying our emotional goodbyes with lots of false promises to return, I trudged my way through the snow for a mile or so to the railway station. On the train to London I remembered the letter in my pocket and took it out. It was indeed from Mrs. Woman's daughter who had also gone to London on an earlier train. She wanted me to meet her at an address in London suggesting, by inference, that we would sleep together. I was more than a little surprised for although we had often socialised together, it had never gone beyond that. I certainly did not realise that I had a secret admirer.

By arrangement, Rene was expecting me at her flat. Her friend was hoping to hear from me about a meeting in London on her return and Mrs. Woman's daughter was hoping that I would arrive at the address that she had given me. I thought to myself, "it never rains but it pours."

Me at 15 Years, before "The Best Twelve Years".    Me (Below) with comrades at Halton. (1941)

Me at Halton aged 16 Years. (1940)

Cyril Woolnough, Our Australian Wartime Captain and Pilot. (1944)

Eric Smith, Our Lancaster Rear Gunner and Myself on his Left. (1944)

ERIC SMITH	MYSELF	CYRIL WOOLNOUGH	IAN RAVENSCROFT	BERT HAGGERSTONE
Sgt. Rear Gunner	Sgt. Flight Engineer	F/O Pilot & Captain	F/O Bomb Aimer	F/Lt. Navigator
Londoner	Colonial	Australian	Canadian	Yorkshireman

HARRY SILZER
Sgt. Midupper Gunner
Canadian

GINGER SMITH
Sgt. Wireless Operator
Scottish

Cousin Pam and I rowing on the Serpentine in Hyde Park London whilst on Leave. (1943)

About to board our Lancaster, dressed for battle. (1944)

An aerial photograph taken after releasing our payload on our mission over Deelan in Holland. (1944)

NOTATION LEGEND

3239 = Lancaster Serial Number
CON. = Conningsby (Our Base)
15.8.44 = Date Of Sortie
8" = Size Of Photograph
17200' = Altitude
←084° = Bombing Run Heading
1208 = Time Of Release
DEELEN A/D = Deelen Airodrome (German Luftwaffe Base In Holland)

11x1000 = 11x 1000 Lb. Bombs
4x500 = 4x 500 Lb. Bombs

C35SECS = Photo Taken 35 Seconds After Bomb Release
F/O WOOLNOUGH = Flying Officer Woolnough (Captain)
E97 = Aircraft Callsign Letter E of 97 Squadron

Max Chivers, Our Pilot on the Berlin Air Lift. (1948)

A Recruitment Brochure that I featured in as "THE ENGINEER".

Men with Wings

Every man who wears R.A.F. wings must be capable of undertaking a task that calls for qualities of the very highest type, both mentally and physically. So, if you are accepted for aircrew duties, you will have the satisfaction of knowing that, judged by Air Force standards—which are probably the most exacting standards in the world—you are rated as a man of outstanding intelligence, character and physique.

In the R.A.F. there are five aircrew categories—Pilot, Navigator, Signaller, Engineer, Gunner. (Note: *The category of Gunner is not at present open to direct entrants.*)

All pilots and navigators who, on entry, are considered suitable to become officers are guaranteed commissions from the start, subject to satisfactory completion of flying and officer training. All others accepted for pilot or navigator training will be given officer cadet status after the 14th week of training and will also be commissioned if they complete the training successfully and reach the standards necessary for commissioned rank.

All signallers, engineers and gunners will have, later on, the opportunity of being considered for permanent commissions in ground branches.

THE NAVIGATOR. *His job is to guide the aircraft to, and bomb the target. He must therefore be an expert in the operation of all navigating instruments and different types of radar.*

THE ENGINEER. *He is responsible for the maintenance of his engines and airframe on the ground and for ensuring that they operate correctly in the air. He must be able to carry out "running repairs" if necessary.*

THE PILOT. *Irrespective of his rank, the pilot is most likely to be captain of his aircraft. The safety of aircraft and crew, the success of every mission depend on his leadership and judgment. He is the key member of the crew.*

THE SIGNALLER. *His job is to maintain communication between his own and other aircraft—and the ground. He must also have a sound knowledge of navigation and bombing aids.*

Our Navigator and myself in India. Although he was an Officer, we still mixed socialy as friends. (1946)

Our Lancastrian crew waiting for our passengers at Queta (Now in Pakistan). (1946)

Me outside my room at RAF Palam India. (1946)

Me below our Lancastrian in India. The strap on my right wrist bore a brass crown the badge of rank for a Warrant Officer.

RAF quarters at Palam India. (1946)

Me (centre) at Brize Norton with Frank Sanders on my right and our comrade known as "The Taylor Bird". (1947)

Attending my good friend Paddy Curtis' Wedding to Dorean his fiancee, along with his comrades at Horsham St. Faith. (1948)

Myself, Pondering a future beyond the RAF. (1950)

7
WAR AND PEACE

We started the year 1945 with 14 days 'end of tour' leave which I spent in London. It was obvious that the war was approaching its end and consequently, the whole apparatus of war was being run down. It was difficult to know what to do with the aircrew who were finishing their required operations and whose number was growing as the opposition declined. One solution was to keep them on leave and so, as soon as we returned from our 'end of tour' fortnight, we were all despatched on further 'indefinite leave.'

Rene had to go into hospital for a small operation and went down to Torquay for a brief convalescence. I, on 'indefinite leave,' accompanied her and to fill our days, she got a job as a secretary in an office whilst I persuaded Mr. Perry, the owner of a large local garage, to employ me unofficially as a semi-skilled motor mechanic at the princely wage of one shilling and ten pence per hour. I had been working there for some time and was expecting soon to be recalled to duty when a job came in for an engine reconditioning. I was given the job of removing the engine and I was less than particular about storing all the bits and pieces that had to be retained whilst the engine was sent to the specialists. To my surprise the engine was back in a few days and I was given the task of reinstalling it. That week most of my pay went on buying all the bits and pieces that I had mislaid.

About the middle of April I got a telegram instructing me to proceed to RAF Leicester East. I travelled almost all day on a cross-country rail journey from Torquay to Leicester Central station and then finally a RAF van to the station headquarters. I then spent the rest of the day going round the various departments getting my arrival documentation signed only to be told, in the end, that my unit, 'the Glider Pick-up Unit,' was at Ibsley, in Hampshire. As a result the whole of the next day was to be spent on another cross-country journey.

The country was experiencing quite a heat wave and I couldn't understand why, every now and then, I would give a cold shudder. By the time I reached my destination I was shivering and so I went straight to the station sick quarters to see the MO (Medical Officer). With a temperature of 104°F (40°c), I was immediately put to bed and given M&B Tablets, May & Baker the manufacturers of early antibiotics. I was diagnosed as having 'Tonsillitis,' which was a surprise, as I had undergone a 'Tonsillectomy' when I was four years old in India.

WAR AND PEACE

During the ten days that I languished in sick quarters the papers were full of ghastly pictures of Belsen concentration camp with its skeleton-like figures, both dead and barely living. The allied armies had crossed the Rhine a few weeks before and were flooding into Germany on all fronts. It was obvious that the war was in its final stage and I was anxious to get out and about in time for the celebrations. When I was declared fit I was sent on ten days convalescent leave in time to read about Field Marshal Montgomery taking the German surrender on Luneburg Heath and finally, the naming of May 8th as 'VE Day' Victory in Europe. Torquay celebrated VE Day as lavishly as any but of course it did not compare with London with its massive crowds around Buckingham Palace and Winston Churchill on the balcony with the Royal Family. To see that we had to wait until we went to the cinema and saw the News Reel. In those days television was just a word we'd heard.

At the end of my convalescent leave I returned to Ibsley and the G.P.U. (Glider Pick-up Unit). The war with Japan had not ended and the GPU was a training unit intended for the jungles of Burma. It consisted of a number of Dakota aircraft each one fitted with a large winch in what would normally be the passenger area. A hydraulically operated boom supported the steel cable that fed from the winch, with a hook for engaging the glider via it's own nylon tow-rope. This nylon rope was held into a giant loop 10 ft. into the air by alloy poles beside the resting glider. The tug aircraft would then swoop down and engage the loop with the hook. A smooth acceleration was achieved by the winch clutch engaging as soon as the tow-rope became taught. Over a period of about five seconds the glider would accelerate from stationary to 120 mph, after which the tug and glider would fly together until the glider decided to release from the tow-rope.

As soon as I realised that Flight Engineers were to be Winch Operators I was most unhappy and immediately started to find a way of getting out of it. Really the way was obvious. I went to see the CO and told him that my family were in Bombay awaiting a passage to England, that I had not seen them for five years and that if I now went to Burma, I may not see them for another five years. The CO was most sympathetic and immediately took me off the course and sent me back on indefinite leave.

Before this took place, however, I had heard from Torquay that two events had occurred. Paddy had returned home from the POW camp in Germany and Rene had returned to London to prepare for the imminent return of her husband from Italy. The Lancasters and Halifaxs of Bomber Command were being used to ferry as many of the troops in Italy as each one could carry to speed up their return home. I immediately obtained a forty-eight hour pass and went to Torquay to see my old friend Paddy after his ordeal. I found him little changed. A bit thinner but with a pint in his hand and a big grin on his face. He had just received all his back pay for the nine months that he had been a prisoner of war, a princely sum, which he seemed determined to exchange with the brewers for their products. I also learned that he had already acquired two girlfriends, both named Margery, who he referred to as Margery Mk.1 and Margery Mk.2. Needless to say, he kept them apart and in ignorance of each other.

On a warm summer's day, whilst waiting for a decision on my next move, I went into Ringwood, our local town in the New Forest. Who should I meet, walking down the street, but Cyril Woolnough, our Lancaster Pilot? We stopped and had a long chat. He told me that he was stationed at nearby RAF Stony Cross flying Stirlings to the middle and Far East. "Just the sort of job I'm after," I thought, "though not particularly on Stirlings." He also told me that he had met a WAAF named Molly with whom he seemed quite smitten. This surprised me a bit because Cyril was never a 'ladies man.' He was a very sociable person and once at Scellkingthorpe he complained that one of the WAAFs in the mess suddenly refused to speak to him. "I can't understand it," he said, "I haven't done anything to her." We all laughed and said, "That's probably why she won't speak to you." Some 38 years later, on a once in a lifetime visit to the UK, Cyril and Molly spent a few days with us. When I reminded Cyril of our meeting in Ringwood he could not remember a thing about it. I said to him, "Don't worry about it Cyril, you were in love."

In the middle of June I received a telegraphed instruction to proceed to Transport Command Head Quarters at Bushy Park in the London area. The previous occupants had been American troops and if they left us nothing else they left us, as graffiti on the cubicle walls, some of the funniest and most colourful rhymes I have heard. It seems that the authorities were at a loss to know what to do with me so they sent me back on indefinite leave. Every time I was asked I said I wanted to fly as an Engineer with Transport Command because I felt, in peacetime, that is where the action would be.

The next attempt at finding me a job took me to 466 squadron at Driffield, in Yorkshire. This was a squadron of Halifax transports used mostly for dropping men and equipment by parachute. At the time they were engaged in taking the ground staff on site seeing trips over Germany to view the damage done by the bombers. Whilst on the squadron I did one flight over the Ruhr at low level and was surprised, myself, at the extent of the damage. Especially Essen, which was totally devastated. The squadron seemed to be over-staffed and so I once again found myself on indefinite leave.

My next posting was to RAF Snaith, also in Yorkshire. This was an appraisal centre where I was to be tested as a potential instructor. Never having tried, I assumed that instructing was easy until my turn came to be tested. I gave an unrehearsed talk on Snakes. It was soon established that lecturing was not my forte. I consoled myself with the belief in George Bernard Shaw's controversial quotation, "He who can, does. He who cannot, teaches." There was, however, one bright spot to my otherwise featureless stay at Snaith. Ginger Smith, the Wireless Operator on our bombing operations at Coningsby, was also being tested. He also failed and we returned to indefinite leave together.

WAR AND PEACE

Whilst waiting for our respective trains, his going north to Scotland, and mine going south to London, we were having a farewell drink in a pub near the railway station. As I passed a table with three people sitting at it I heard a crash and looking down, I saw that a drink had been spilt. I felt sure that I had not knocked it over but acting the perfect gentleman, I apologised and offered to buy another. To my surprise my offer was accepted and on my return with the drink I was invited to join them. I agreed, and I soon found myself paired off with one of the attractive girls in the group. Next, I was invited to accompany them home, which I did, as it seemed like a good adventure. There I found that the girl was a visitor from London and two days later we both got on the train together still a little drink sodden, having spent most of our time in pubs. As soon as we got off the train at Kings Cross the girl walked away with hardly a goodbye and we never saw each other again. This was typical however, of how strangers would interact during these times.

Paddy's brother Des was on leave in London at the time and I joined him. After a few days I found the old Tonsillitis symptoms returning and so I took myself off to Hendon which was still an active RAF station. There I reported to the sick quarters, saw the MO and was immediately admitted. It was early August and as I lay in bed reading the papers, I was surprised to learn that a new super weapon called the 'Atom Bomb' had been dropped on Hiroshima, a Japanese city, with devastating results. This seemed to bring no response from the Japanese government. Just before I was discharged from the sick quarters, I read that another similar bomb had been dropped on Nagasaki. Shortly after that, the Japanese had agreed to unconditional surrender and the official date had been set for the 15th August. This was VJ Day, Victory over Japan.

On the day in question I found myself still on leave, but alone in London (Des had returned to duty). I went out to join the celebrations and whilst drinking in a pub, I was approached by a member of a celebrating group who explained that they were about to go on to a party in someone's flat and would I like to join them? This was an offer too good to refuse and I soon found myself in high spirits with a crowd of total strangers who seemed to accept me as one of them.

From London, I carried on down to Torquay to continue my indefinite leave where, shortly after, I was told to report to an Army Hospital in a delightful part of rural Devon. There I was to undergo another Tonsillectomy. As previously mentioned, I was alleged to have had my Tonsils out at aged four, in India, where I could still remember being anaesthetised with a chloroform mask. Now the specialist's report stated, 'Left Tonsil - swollen, Right Tonsil - ragged remains.' So much for medicine in India in the nineteen twenties. I was operated on the day after I was admitted and expected to spend two weeks on the ward. However, I felt very well and surprised the medics by asking if I could eat the day after the operation. This was in contrast to another patient who had undergone a Tonsillectomy and who proved, unexpectedly, to be a Haemophiliac. Every time they removed the clamps he bled profusely. They finally managed to stop the bleeding by the use of 'Viper Venom.' Every day that we were in hospital we received a bottle of Guinness. I decided to save mine and as a result of my pestering, I was allowed to leave after ten days with ten bottles of Guinness which I used for a mini party.

I was barely back to fighting fit again when I heard that my family had arrived in England and were staying with Mrs. Miles in Twickenham. About the same time I was notified by the RAF that I had been promoted to Warrant Officer. I hastened up to London and to Twickenham, where I confronted my family with the strangest emotions. They seemed like strangers to me and I found myself, while talking to my sister, referring to our mother as "your mother." I did wonder if my father felt proud of me, after only five years, becoming a Warrant Officer, the highest non-commissioned rank in the service. I didn't tell him that promotions for flying aircrew were automatic and annual.

As the family had no solid roots in England I tried to persuade them that Torquay was a very pleasant place in which to settle. They agreed to have a look at it and before long, with Paddy's mothers help, they were ensconced as lodgers in two nearby houses. They stayed there until after Christmas when my father, because he was unable to get a suitable engineering job in Torquay, took himself off to Birmingham. There he made contact with the Lines family, relations of his, whom I had never heard of. Co-incidentally, they were also looking for accommodation and the two families agreed to share a large rented house on Gravely Hill, Erdington, until each was in a position to buy something more permanent.

Meanwhile, in early December I was, at last, recalled to permanent duty. I was sent to RAF Full Sutton, near York, now the venue of a high security prison. I was to join 232 Squadron which was being reformed and fitted out with Lancastrian aircraft. This was the civil version of the Lancaster bomber without gun turrets and with a nose cone and a pointed tail in place of the two turrets at the extremities. A single 1,000 gallon petrol tank was sealed in what had previously been the bomb bay. This gave it a range of some 3,000 miles, a considerable improvement on most piston-engined aircraft of the time. We were told that the purpose of the squadron was to replace the American 'Skymasters' that were currently flying from Ceylon (Sri Lanka) to Sydney, in Australia. Keeping the air routes open until the civil airlines could take over. The Skymasters had been obtained on 'Lease Lend' and were to be returned to the USA.

This seemed the very answer to my wanderlust and I settled down to enjoy my future prospects. The training went on for some three months as most of my colleagues were new to Lancasters or Lancastrians and the aircraft were arriving from the factory a lot slower than they did during the war. In February, the weather turned bitterly cold and as Full Sutton was a war emergency airfield, we were billeted in Nissan huts. We always said that the Nissan huts were fitted with 'central heating' as the only heating was a tall cast-iron stove in the centre of the hut. During the evening we would all huddle round the stove and try to out-do each other with our 'tales of the unexpected.' The one that amused us most was the lad who explained that the gas from a fart was pure methane and to prove it, he turned on his back and with bent legs astride in the air and a flaming cigarette lighter held near his arse, he blew an enormous fart. It was the nearest thing to a flame thrower and we all gave him the applause he deserved.

Shortly after bedtime, the stove went out and the room went into deep freeze. Even though I slept in my clothes, except for my trousers, which were laid out under me to give them a crease, I was still cold. I tried putting newspaper between the blankets but, though they crackled loudly every time I turned over, they were not the answer. 'The final solution' came when I made myself an electric fire out of a small sheet of aluminium, a length of flex and a tubular element, which I had to buy. This I plugged into the light fitting above my bed and ran it all night. I did explain to my roommates that it was a fire risk but that if it did cause a fire, we would at least have a real warm room for a while.

Perhaps the only event of note, during the flying programme, took place one morning when I had to take an aircraft on a test flight with a Pilot. For some reason I wasn't in a particularly good mood that morning. Perhaps somebody had spoken to me before breakfast. I was told that I would have to join the crew that were to fly the aircraft which did nothing to lift my spirits. As the new crew were entering the aircraft, a voice said "Everything OK Engineer?" "Yeare" I growled in reply, then noticed the forage cap that had been thrown down on the seat near me. It had blue braiding on it, an indication that it belonged to an Officer of air rank. That is, an Air Commodore or above. "SIR," I added emphatically.

The Air Commodore was to be the Pilot but I noticed that he only had one arm. His right arm was a stump ending at the elbow. I recognised him immediately. It was the legendary 'Gus Walker.' Some years before, he had been running towards a blazing aircraft on the ground to help the crew, when the plane exploded, seriously injuring him and resulting in the amputation of his right arm. I watched, with interest as he took the right hand Pilot's seat rather than the traditional left. He had, fixed to the stub of his right arm, a device with a clamp on the end, which he screwed to the control wheel leaving his left hand free to operate all the controls located between the two Pilots. He also took the precaution of carrying with him a safety Pilot.

As we took off I had no idea what the exercise was to be but we climbed and headed west for about an hour. As we flew over Morecambe Bay I realised that we were heading for Northern Ireland and while listening to the R.T. (Radio Telephone) conversation, learned that we were about to land at RAF Nutts Corner.

The two Pilots left us and disappeared into the maize of buildings on the station. They returned about an hour later with a couple of dead chickens and about a dozen eggs, complete luxuries in England at that time. We then took off and returned to Full Sutton. When we landed Gus Walker thanked the crew and disappeared with his spoils. The next

WAR AND PEACE

time I saw him was some fifteen years later when we were both civilians. I was at the Leicester Tigers rugby ground, waiting to see them play one of their principle adversaries. Suddenly, from out of the 'tunnel' ran a solitary figure, his stump waving in place of his right arm. It was Gus Walker, the referee.

The squadron had just started to be formed into crews. The intention was for two crews to take each Lancastrian out to India and the first two crews had been selected. My own position in the queue was suddenly enhanced by the intervention of Rene's husband, John. I had seen Rene again at Christmas. She was having difficulty in readjusting to her marriage and our affair had resurrected itself on a sporadic basis. John, who was a recently demobbed Army Captain, decided to don his Officer's uniform and to go up to Full Sutton and have a 'man to man' with my Commanding Officer. The result of this was that my CO sent for me and told me that he was putting me in one of the first two crews to go and that I would be leaving within a week. He was as good as his word and within a few days I was heading for RAF Pershore, in Worcestershire, to await the arrival of our operational Lancastrians. The first two crews had not yet left and were entertaining themselves with nights out in nearby Birmingham. The next thing that we heard was that one of the Flight Engineers in the initial crews had contracted gonorrhoea in Birmingham and I was selected to replace him. I now found myself in the first plane to go and we were soon flying down to RAF St. Mawgan, in Cornwall, our departure base.

8
INDIA REVISITED

We were due to take off at nine o'clock the following evening and before then, I wrote my mother a long letter in which I said that, by the time she received the letter, I would be in India. A truly amazing state of affairs for the time. No more than six months previously the family had taken the normal three weeks for the voyage by sea and as yet there was no air route to India. As there were two crews we tossed a coin to see which crew would fly the first leg. I don't know whether we won or lost but we slept the first leg. The Lancastrian would never have made a profit as a commercial airliner, though British South American Airways, under Donald Bennett, the wartime Pathfinder boss, did operate them for a short while. The fuselage, to the rear of the main spar, contained accommodation for twelve passengers seated in a single row facing sideways or six sleeping lengthwise in two rows of three each, one above the other.

As the flying crew took up their working stations we, the second crew, took up our sleeping positions. I was not used to being a passenger and as I lay on my bunk, I could not help from wondering if the Engineer had remembered to do this, that and the other and it was not until we had settled down at cruising altitude, about 10,000 ft., that I was able to relax and soon went fast asleep.

I awoke to find, in broad daylight, that we were crossing a barren coastline from an azure sea. I soon realised that we were flying over Libya from the amount of war wreckage that was strewn all over the area. There were burned out aircraft, tanks, lorries and all manner of military hardware, which were slowly rotting away in the desert. We flew over this barren landscape for another two hours before we started to lose height and finally landed at an airfield in the desert. It was RAF Cairo West and very much west too, as it was some 50 miles west of Cairo, without a scrap of vegetation in sight. We went straight into breakfast where we were waited on by a retinue of gowned and fezzed waiters. It felt almost as if we had landed on another planet.

As soon as we were fed and the plane refuelled we took off. It was good to feel the 'reins in my hands' again and we flew non-stop to Karachi, where we landed at four o'clock in the morning. This was another feeding and refuelling stop and we took advantage of the break to have a much-needed wash and brush up. Whilst in the ablutions I mislaid some items of my toiletry and spotting the Indian cleaner, I approached him with the intention of asking him, in his own language, if he had seen them. I opened my mouth to speak, but nothing seemed to come out. The Urdu language, that I spoke reasonably well before I left India, now seemed to escape me. I determined to make a conscious effort to rectify this. Urdu.was, more or less, the 'lingua franca' of the Indian sub-continent and would be useful wherever I was based.

We took off from Karachi in darkness and some three and a half hours later, landed at RAF Palam, now Delhi International Airport. After six years in the RAF at some fifteen different locations, I could rarely, now, visit any RAF station, anywhere in the world, without meeting somebody that I knew and Palam was no exception. Amongst the small group that had come onto the tarmac to welcome us, I spotted a couple of old colleagues and leaning out of the window, I shouted a jokingly rude greeting. Then they gave us the bad news. "The squadron was disbanded yesterday," they said. "Why?" we asked. "The air lines are ready to take over," was the reply. "Oh well," we said, "Presumably we turn round and go back home again." "Not likely," was the response, "You've just brought us the very plane we need, a long range aircraft suitable for carrying VIPs." This made us realise that we were talking to members of 'A.H.Q.I. Communications squadron' which stood for Air Headquarters, India, to which we were about to be seconded. The function of the 'Comm. Squadron' was to provide air transport for all the high-ranking members of the various military headquarters, along with the Viceroy's staff, all of who were located in New Delhi.

We were allocated a room each from a row of rooms with a common veranda. Each consisted of a single room about 15ft. square with a ceiling-mounted electric fan in the centre, a front and rear door and a small annex at the back containing a cold water shower. The water in most parts of India was never cold enough to be uncomfortable. Hot water systems were practically unknown. The furniture consisted of a dressing table-cum-writing desk and a 'Charpoy'. Charpoy was the Urdu word for bed, and consisted of a rectangular wooden frame with four legs and the frame closely strung with choir rope. My room was at the end of the block and my two neighbours were both Flight Engineers who had been made redundant as they had qualified too late for operational flying and had not been in the RAF long enough for early release. They both had ground jobs. It was not long before I realised that there were a large number of redundant aircrew on the station in similar circumstances. Although some of them had somewhat menial tasks, they were all allowed to retain their Sergeant's stripes and pay. My two neighbours and myself shared a servant between us, known as a 'bearer,' to whom we each paid 4 rupees (30p) per week.

As there did not seem to be any prospect of much action in the near future and while there were still two crews qualified to fly the Lancastrian, I thought it might be an opportunity to visit my old haunts in Bombay. So I went to see the CO and told him that my sister, whom I had not seen for six years, was in Bombay, awaiting a ship to take her to England. Before I could say any more he sent for his orderly and said, "Book Warrant Officer Gould on a flight to Bombay on

INDIA REVISITED

Tata Air Lines returning in one week". I couldn't have asked for more. I soon began to realise that my CV (ex Halton Apprentice with two Operational Tours with Path Finders) would gain me a few privileges, though I never abused this. Within a few days I was driven to Willingden Air-port, the civic airport for Delhi at that time, and was winging my way towards Bombay.

In Bombay, I stayed with my Uncle John who had a flat not far from the famous 'Gateway of India' arch. My sister, Rosalie, was also staying there, awaiting her ship to England. When the rest of the family had sailed, the previous year, she had stayed behind to finish her teachers training course. She was occupying the guest room so I slept on a camp bed in the living room. I was awakened the next morning, by a six-year-old girl who had crawled under the camp bed and was pushing it up with her feet, screaming with excitement. This was my introduction to my cousin, Christine, who had been born shortly after I left India in 1940.

The first thing I did that day was to contact my cousin, Frank, who as a virtual orphan, had been brought up by my parents, as one of our family. As children, he and I had been very close, more like brothers. He was awaiting his discharge from the Indian Army and a passage to England. He had a small flat in a block belonging to the Army and I moved in with him. I found myself 'living it up' with many of my old school friends and one night, as a small group of us were walking along one of the main streets, with a few drinks in us, we were approached by an Indian pimp. "Bibi sahib," he said, "Pucka Anglo Indian bibi almost virgin." He couldn't understand why we all fell about with laughter. We revisited most of our old haunts including our old school, 'the Cathedral,' and found that they had hardly changed at all during the war years. I voted it the best weeks leave I had ever spent.

I returned to Delhi to find that the other crew that had come out with us, had gone to Ceylon to collect the last 'Skymaster' that had now been restored to serviceability and was ready to go back to the USA. Worse than that, the other Engineer was qualified on Skymasters and was the obvious choice to take it. They brought the plane back to Delhi where it stood on the tarmac for almost a week while the necessary formalities were gone through. I heard that its flight was to be routed through the UK and I got my colleague to agree to take a parcel and post it in England. I knew that my mother was very partial to mangoes, which were absolutely unobtainable at home, so I thought I would give her a treat. I bought half a dozen green mangoes and made them into a secure parcel which I placed in the aircraft on the morning of its departure. Unfortunately its departure was delayed for twenty-four hours while they stood, motionless, in the blazing sun. When my mother received them she wrote and thanked me politely but said that, by that time, the mangoes were all 'over-ripe'.

Now that our second crew had departed we were left in sole charge of our Lancastrian. It was the middle of April and the weather was getting extremely hot. To ensure the continued serviceability of the aircraft and more urgently, to obtain respite from the midday heat, we would take the plane up on air test every few days. Sometimes on these flights we would go up to 10,000 ft. where we would cruise around for an hour enjoying the cool air. On one such occasion we flew to nearby Agra and circled low over the Taj Mahal.

Before long, we were given our first task. Air Commodore Jarmin wished to attend a conference in Cairo. He also wished to be away for the shortest possible time. Consequently, with him and his aides on board and a full load of fuel, we took off at nine o'clock at night, flew for fourteen and a half hours, mostly against light head winds, and landed at nine thirty, local time, the following morning. Our passengers left the aircraft as sprightly as spring chickens having slept all night on the bunks. For the crew, on the other hand, it was different. With our heads swimming from a combination of blazing sunshine and fatigue, we staggered to the nearby Helliopilus Grand Palace Hotel, which had been commandeered for transit accommodation. There we caught up with our sleep soon enough to go into Cairo in the early evening. The next night we took off for Delhi. The return flight only took thirteen hours with the benefit of tail winds.

By May, the weather was even hotter. Too hot, the authorities felt, for the few remaining WAAFs that were still in India. We were given the job of transferring them to Ceylon and with a contingent of nine on board, we flew down to RAF Negombo, a single runway cut out of the coconut tree forest some 18 miles north of Colombo, the capital. A few days later we flew down to RAF Santa Cruise, now Bombay

International Airport, picked up the remaining five girls and delivered them to Negombo, returning the next day with ten male passengers.

Towards the end of the month we were told that Field Marshal Wavel, the Viceroy, was thinking of attending the Victory Parade in London. The Lancastrian was his only viable means of getting there. However, the Lancastrian was due for a 30-hour inspection and even the King himself did not have the authority to order into the air an aircraft that was due for an inspection. For the trip to take place it was necessary for the inspection to be done immediately and so I set out to organise this. To hasten things along I carried out much of the work myself which was well on the way to completion by lunchtime. This was the end of the working day in the hot summer. However, whilst waiting for lunch in the Sergeant's Mess, I began to feel quite nauseous and Doug Manton, our Wireless Operator, who had been in South East Asia for the last three years, gave me an instant diagnosis of 'heat exhaustion' and immediately took me to sick quarters. There I was given two jugs of salt water to drink which I downed with no difficulty. I was then admitted to the sick quarters and put to bed for three days by which time it was too late for the Viceroy to attend the parade.

June was the hottest month, just before the monsoons cooled things slightly. On the hottest night in June I was at a loss to know how to handle the heat. Normally I slept under the 'Punka' the electric ceiling fan, without a mosquito net. I kept perspiring so I took my bed out into the veranda. But, as I could be seen, I had to put up the mosquito net. This was worse so I took it further out hoping to catch a breath of breeze. There was none so I went back under the fan but before lying on the bed, I got under the cold shower and dripping wet, I lay under the fan which cooled me enough for me to sleep for a couple of hours. I awoke in a sweat and had to repeat the procedure to get me through the night.

As soon as it got known that I was able to speak Urdu I became the unofficial camp interpreter. One day, when I was down at the servicing area, the 'Chiefy' came up to me and said, "Hay Gouldy, do us a favour. Those coolies are supposed to be cleaning that Dakota, but they're just sitting on their arses pretending not to know what I'm talking about. Could you sort them out for me?" I went into the aircraft and spoke sharply to them in Urdu at which they leapt to their feet in amazement and started working furiously. On another occasion I was inveigled into taking part in a practical joke that had a regrettable conclusion. There was an Indian hawker who had permission to sell fruit on the camp. He would walk around with a springy stride and a basket of fruit on his head calling out, in a falsetto voice, "Lovely Cherry Plumbs." My colleagues got hold of him one day and using me as an interpreter, offered to teach him a new call that would increase his sales. After drilling him for about an hour, they watched with interest, as he strode off, his basket on his head, and with his jaunty walk, shouting, in his high pitched voice, "Fuckin Arseholes!" Unfortunately the Station Warrant Officer's wife lived on the camp and she objected, resulting in him losing his franchise.

The use of the Lancastrian, for official purposes, was very sparing and we had to find various ways of filling our idle time. One little hobby that I pursued was reading. I decided to try and increase my vocabulary by getting the most intellectually 'upmarket' books that I could find in the library. Classics like 'The Cloister and the Hearth', though 'The Complete works of Shakespeare' was my constant companion. I read these books with an English Dictionary always open by my side. As another diversion I even tried to organise a water-polo match in an unofficial swimming area in the neighbouring cantonment. When we had to make one player a goalkeeper because he couldn't swim, I realised that water polo was too esoteric a sport and when I got a very painful boil in the ear from the swimming, the whole idea was abandoned.

Not long after this I had a bout of Enteritis, common in the tropics. In Egypt it was known as 'Gypo Tummy' and in India, as 'Bombay Tummy.' I spent all day lying on my bed with frequent visits to the loo. By evening I was able to summon up enough energy to visit the Sick Quarters. I had to wait for the MO to finish his game of squash. When he entered, in boisterous mood, I told him my problem and he said, "What would you like me to do?" "Give me some medicine," I replied. "What colour medicine?" "Blue is my favourite colour." I was beginning to enter into the spirit of the thing. "Blue is poison," he said, "I'll give you a dose of Caster Oil. That'll clear you out." It did the trick and after that Caster Oil became my panacea for all tummy upsets.

For some time I had been worried about hair loss. My uncle

INDIA REVISITED

John had been completely bald in his thirties and I thought I could be heading the same way. I considered shaving my head to strengthen the growth. The main reason that I rejected this was because, in India, a shorn head symbolised grief for a deceased loved one. Instead I started using Coconut Oil as a hair dressing. When I eventually returned to the UK I found that the Coconut Oil had solidified in the colder climate. I then decided to replace it with Caster Oil, so I now had a common remedy for hair loss as well as tummy troubles.

I also noticed that the hair on my upper lip was more robust than that on my chin, so I decided to grow a moustache and shave my chin to strengthen the growth. There were strict rules governing facial hair in the British Armed Forces. The Army and the RAF were allowed to wear a moustache but not a beard. The Navy, on the other hand, could only wear a moustache if accompanied by a beard. Several of my comrades were content to let the Indian barber shave them in bed each morning before they woke up. Personally, I could never bring myself to quite trust a man wielding an open cutthroat razor so near my exposed throat.

In August the RAF decided to mount an attempt on the air speed record from England to New Zealand. Personnel from the 'Empire Air Navigation School' were to crew a Lancastrian. This would be an official attempt and would certainly sweep away our unofficial record from England to India. They had a scheduled refuelling stop at RAF St. Thomas' Mount, Madras, and we were instructed to fly down to this air field to await their landing and to standby to act as a 'Christmas Tree.' This meant that, if any spare parts were required at that stage, they would be taken off our Lancastrian which would be left stranded until the replacement part could be sent out from England. We prayed hard and our prayers were answered. The plane came and went on and we returned to Delhi. The record didn't last long. Twenty years later, jet powered airliners were doing better every day.

It was about this time that I heard that my cousin Frank had been discharged from the Indian Army and was awaiting a passage to England. I took a few days off when I heard that there was a Dakota going down to Bombay and cadged a lift in it. As he was not about to sail we decided that he could have a few days in Delhi with me. We also decided to take his pushbike with us. The Pilot raised no objection to any of this and some six hours later, Frank was safely ensconced in my room. Unfortunately there was not another flight to Bombay scheduled in the foreseeable future and Frank had to return by train, leaving his cycle to me. I saw him off at the railway station feeling a little guilty that I was not able to get him a return flight. It would now take him twenty-four hours to get to Bombay instead of the five hours that the flight took.

One of my many friends on the camp was the Sergeant clerk in charge of the orderly room. He was an ex boy clerk, trained at Ruislip, the Halton equivalent of the administration service. He came to me, one day, and said, "Did you know that you can shorten your service and double your gratuity?" "How?" I asked. "By getting on the Bounty

Scheme," he replied. "Don't be daft," I said, "You know I'm an ex-brat on a regular engagement. I've got another seven years to go." "It doesn't matter," he went on, "I've studied the relative document and it's open to all non-commissioned aircrew and does not preclude regulars. Take my word for it you'll be all right. After all what've you got to loose?" The Bounty Scheme was not intended to be open to regulars, it was an administrative lapse when the scheme was drafted. It was meant to offer selected aircrew, on 'hostilities only' engagements, the opportunity to defer their discharge by three years, with four years on the reserve, and to receive a £200 gratuity, £25 at the start, and £175 on completion of the three years. Furthermore there would be an opportunity, when the three years were up, to extend my service, if I wished, for an indeterminate period. Here was an offer I could hardly refuse and I put in my application straight away and awaited the inevitable boards.

Whilst waiting for my board we did a couple of short trips within the Indian borders. One was to RAF Dum Dum, Calcutta. This trip was notable for two things. On the way there, flying above the haze layer, we could see, at a distance of 200 miles, three tiny peaks that looked like three little teeth. The Navigator assured us that the central one was Mount Everest. The other thing was at Dum Dum where the transit accommodation was in a somewhat dilapidated condition. The partitions that formed the cubicles in the toilet block had been demolished and had not yet been renewed. Consequently going to the loo became a social occasion. As I sat on my 'throne' I noticed that my neighbour was an old Halton friend. That started us on quite an animated conversation which was listened to, with interest, by the rest of the occupants.

The other trip was to RAF Quetta, at the head of the Bolan Pass, the alternative to the famous Khyber Pass, as a way into Afghanistan. It was an awe-inspiring flight as we cruised along the pass at 10,000 ft. with the mountains towering above us. We had, as passengers, a small party of VIPs who were attending a meeting. Whilst the meeting was taking place the crew, along with one or two 'hangers on', were sitting in the shade of the aircraft when a couple of Pathans, the local hill tribesmen, came past. They stopped and one of them addressed us in Pushdu, the local dialect. Getting a blank response he tried Urdu which brought an immediate reaction from me. We had a long chat, mostly about the aircraft and its size, with which he was mightily impressed. As soon as they had taken their leave one of the 'hangers on' in our party turned to me and said, "You've picked up the language quick. You haven't been here very long, have you?" "It's a gift," I said, nonchalantly. The laughter from the others ruined the whole effect.

Before long I was told that I had to go to RAF Barrackpore, near Calcutta, for my 'Bounty Scheme' board. There were about half a dozen of us altogether and we all flew there in a Dakota, one of the frequent flights between Delhi and Calcutta. One of the applicants was Doug. Manton, our Wireless Operator, so naturally we did everything together. This included a night out in Calcutta where we found our way into a nightclub that was full of service personnel and more girls than I had yet seen in India. I noticed a soldier who had two attractive girls with him. When he went to the loo I followed him. "You've got your hands full," I said. "Yes," he replied, "Would you like to take one off me?" "OK," I said and went back to his table with him where he introduced me to the girls. The next morning I was at Calcutta's main railway station to catch a train back to Barrackpore when who should I bump into? but Doug Manton, glowing with pride and anxious to tell me about his last night's experience.

Doug and I were the last to complete our board, having to return after lunch. The others were off before lunch and waving their railway warrants in the air, they dashed off to the railway station intending to catch an earlier train than us. When Doug and I were finished we didn't bother with our railway warrant to Delhi. We caught a train going in another direction. We went to Dum Dum instead. There we found a Dakota almost ready to leave for Delhi. We had no difficulty in being accepted aboard and by the end of the day we were back in our billets. The next afternoon, after lunch, we were sitting on the veranda of the mess sipping a cool drink, when a small party of travel-weary airmen came past. They were the ones who had dashed off to catch the earlier train and had just arrived back at camp, twenty- four hours later.

The NAAFI, which was responsible for victualling the home forces elsewhere, did not operate on the Indian sub-continent. Indian contractors were used instead. Because at that time most of the British had not acquired a taste for curry, it was never served in the mess. On the other hand I had been weaned on curry and in the hot weather, I began to suffer withdrawal systems. To get 'a fix,' I would do one of two things. Sometimes I would pay a visit to John Dickinson, a second or third cousin, once or twice removed, on my Grandmother's side, who worked for the Indian Civil Service, and lived in a spacious bungalow in New Delhi. We invariably had curry for dinner after which he would run me into Conaught Circus in the sidecar of his motorcycle to catch the RAF transport back to camp. More often I would go to a restaurant with a couple of colleagues whose tastes I was attempting to refine. Old Delhi, the original Indian city, was a crowded, squalid area, to be avoided unless a visit was essential. New Delhi, on the other hand, had not evolved like most cities. It had been designed by British architects, with a matrix of straight intersecting streets appended by the Viceroy's palace which was grouped around by the various buildings of state. Elsewhere lay Conaught Circus, the shopping and social area, where life appeared to cease after midnight. New Delhi was rightly described as 'a city without a soul.'

When we went into New Delhi in the afternoon we invariably called at the Wavel club. This was a newly built establishment with a swimming pool where we could get some relief from the heat and relax in the shade of the trees. Sometimes we went shopping in the evening. To get some refreshment, and to distance ourselves from the Street Hawkers, the Fortune-Tellers, the Ear Pickers, Beggars, Jadoo Wallas (magicians) who doubled as Snake Charmers, and the Shoeshine boys who, if you didn't let them polish your shoes, would throw dirt on them. To get away from all this we would visit the carpet shop. Here the ritual was always the same. On entering, we were placed in a raised wooden arm chair, given a much needed cup of tea and invited to view the large selection of carpets that were displayed, one at a time, by a small army of lackeys. The fact that we never bought anything did not seem to deter them from putting on a repeat performance for our next visit.

On a night out, with my friend, Peter Payne, we didn't relish another early night so we ignored the last liberty wagon, as the truck was called that took us into town and back. In New Delhi one could only get a beer with a meal. Having sat drinking after our curry, until the restaurant closed at mid-night, we felt that we had drunk just about enough to want more. "Let's go to the restaurant at the railway station," I said. "It'll be closed," Peter replied. "They never close," I concluded, "Let's go." We hailed a 'Tonga' and climbed aboard. A Tonga was a two wheeled, horse drawn vehicle that plied for hire. It had two back-to-back seats and could carry up to four passengers, three in the back and one, alongside the driver in the front. The railway station was in the old city and it did not take us long to get there. We found the restaurant closed and in darkness. Undeterred, we knocked continuously on the glazed entrance door until we saw a figure rise up from the floor between the tables. It was the night waiter. He switched on the lights, opened the door and proceeded to lay a table for us. By the time we had drunk three or four large bottles of beer, without a meal, it was getting late. As soon as we left, the waiter switched off the lights and returned to his position on the floor between the tables.

We were now faced with a 15 mile return trip to camp. The obvious choice was a taxi and we started negotiations with the taxi drivers, most of whom could speak a little English. We compared the figure that they were asking with the total amount of cash that we had left and found that we had a mismatch. So we turned our attention to the Tongas. The Tonga Wallas, as the drivers were called, mostly couldn't speak any English. Once again I came into my own. We found a Tonga Walla who was so amazed at being able to bargain with an Englishman in his own language that he cheerfully agreed to do what to him, was a round trip of 30 miles. But first he had to change his horse.

He returned in about half an hour with a sprightly steed and we set off. The journey took about an hour and when we found that we were out of cigarettes, he was quite happy to share his 'Beedees' with us. Beedees were what most of the Indians smoked. They consisted of finely chopped leaves that looked like tobacco but smelled like something else. These were wrapped in a single, brown, dried leaf and tied, in the middle, with a piece of string. If they had been the only tobacco available we would soon have been free of our smoking addiction.

Another friend of mine was a Sergeant Pilot who's surname was Sparrow. He was known as 'Spadge.' He had obtained his wings too late in the war to do any operational flying and now had a ground job. One evening he and I returned from a night out in New Delhi feeling quite 'Peckish.' "Let's go to Spencer's Restaurant," he suggested. In preparation for Palam becoming an International Airport, a small Terminal Building had been built with a restaurant run by an Indian firm by the name of Spencer. "I haven't enough money for a meal there," I replied. "Spencer's will give us credit," he added. I did not question this as I assumed that he knew something that I did not.

We sat down at a table in the empty restaurant and the night-waiter took our order. When he asked us it we wanted anything to drink we said "No." At the conclusion of our meal Spadge ordered coffees. As soon as the waiter disappeared into the kitchen Spadge said, "Come on, let's get going," and we rushed out into the darkness. "It's alright for him," I thought, "He need never come in here again." On the other hand, every time we had an early take off, we would have breakfast at Spencer's. Consequently I lived in fear of being recognised for some time after.

A short while later, Spadge took a few days 'French Leave' (the popular term for unauthorised leave) and went off to Karachi to escape the boredom of Delhi. On his return, as an intended punishment, he was put in charge of the Technical Store. However, I suppose I should not really have been surprised when he then invited me to come in and be kitted out with my own personal tool-kit complete with leather tool bag.

For the last several months a trio of Labour Government Ministers had been negotiating with the Indian leaders, arrangements for the transfer of power to an all-Indian government. Throughout the two hundred years of the 'British Raj' there had been friction between the Hindu majority and the very large minority of Muslims. A relatively small incident could spark a full scale riot which had to be broken up by the British led Indian police, using 'Lathis' as their wooden staves were called. On the rare occasions when the police were unable to gain control, British soldiers, with fixed bayonets, supported them. Gandhi passionately wanted the two religions to live together in harmony, but Jinna, the leader of the Muslim league, had his mind set on partition. He wanted two nations, Hindustan, the land of the Hindus, and Pakistan, the land of the pure. Ultimately he got his way except that the Hindus kept the name India in preference to Hindustan, possibly we thought, as a snub to the Muslims for considering themselves pure.

The number of servicemen in India was gradually being reduced as those on wartime engagements were returning to the UK for demob. One of these was our second Pilot with whom I shared an interest in photography. Only a few days before he left for Bombay to catch the boat he and I were developing films together in an improvised dark-room, with blankets covering the doors and windows. About a week after he left we were told that he had died in Bombay, of Poliomyelitis. These were the days before the Salk vaccine and little was understood about the disease. I and the rest of the crew were given a course of nose drops and gargles

INDIA REVISITED

and much touching of wood. Miraculously we all remained unscathed.

Another airman had his repatriation and demob. put in jeopardy when he found himself on a murder charge. He had been out in the bush hunting game with a 303in. Lee Enfield, Service rifle. He was stalking some prey when he heard a rustle in the bushes. He turned on it and fired. Unfortunately it turned out to be an Indian who had been taken short and had squatted down behind the bush. His shot had killed the man. By pleading guilty to a lesser charge, he was convicted of manslaughter, and sentenced, by an Indian judge, to be fined 600 rupees (£45). The alternative to the fine was six months rigorous imprisonment. There was no way any one of us could have paid a fine of £45, a huge sum in those days. Consequently, a collection was made for him from the whole camp and the money raised. The fine was paid and he went off to Bombay to catch the boat.

In November we set off on a trip to Singapore with an overnight stop at Dum Dum, Calcutta, on the way. We landed at RAF Changi, in Singapore now the International Air Port, and also the location of its notorious jail. As we had only two days in Singapore we lost no time in going into town to explore. Brown skinned Orientals who looked better built than the average natives manned the main-gate. When I asked who they were, I was told that they were Japanese prisoners of war. That explains why they bowed from the waist as we drove out, I thought. Later that evening I went into the Sergeant's Mess for a beer and was surprised to meet none other than the boy, now a man, who I had the bare knuckle fight with at Halton six years previously. We greeted each other like long lost friends and spent the evening reminiscing over glasses of beer. On the return trip we called at RAF Mingaladon, Rangoon, the capital of Burma. As we taxied in I noticed that the man who was guiding us in with the 'ping-pong bats' was the 'Chiefy' in charge of Servicing with 61 squadron at Coningsby and Skellingthorpe in 1944. As the RAF got smaller I seemed to meet old friends all over the world.

Four days after our return we had a surprise visit from a unit that we had never heard of. It was called 'The Transport Command Examining Unit'. It consisted of a complete crew of highly qualified aircrew Officers whose job it was to test every member of the crew and award each a categorisation letter that represented a percentage mark. The final category of the person being tested was the lowest percentage achieved in any one subject. If a person achieved a category of less than 'B,' which was 80%-90%, they would have to take another test in six months. 'A' or 'B' categories lasted twelve months. As part of my test I was blindfolded and the name of a control or component was called out. I was expected to put my hand straight on it without any groping or fumbling. At the end of the test I was relieved to hear that I had been awarded a 'B' category.

Our flying activities now seemed to be slowly grinding to a halt. At the same time my self-improvement activities increased. To give myself a break I would occasionally spend the evening having a drink in the Sergeant's Mess. One night, on returning to my room, I found a snake curled up under my bed. I recognised it at once as a 'Crate,' a small, poisonous, though somewhat sluggish snake. I edged along the wall to the corner and grasped the pole that was used for operating the skylight. I pushed the very light bed clear of the snake and then broke it's back with the pole. I scooped the dead snake out into the gutter at the back. The next morning all that remained in the gutter was a small bloodstain. No doubt the vultures had spotted it. There was always a line of vultures perched on the kitchen roof waiting for scraps.

In mid-December, we were told that we would be returning to the UK shortly after Christmas. This was the best news that we had received since we had been in the country. India, and especially Delhi, was no place for a healthy young man with aspirations to an active social life. Our 'bearer,' on the other hand, was most displeased to hear the news. I had become a bit of a favourite with him, not only because I could speak his language, but also because when he brought us a curry that his wife had made, I eagerly ate the lion's share of it.

A warm Christmas was a new experience to most of my comrades but I, personally, preferred them. I always felt that snow scenes looked better on Christmas cards than in real life. The four of us, who the bearer worked for, clubbed together to give him a generous Christmas box and when we asked him if he intended to buy his wife a present he surprised us by telling us that he intended to spend it in the brothel. "But you have a wife on the camp," we said, "and also another at your 'muluck' (home town)". "Too many 'butcha' (children)," he replied, shaking his head. As a farewell present, just before we left, I gave him the bicycle that Frank had left me when he sailed for home. This was almost the equivalent of giving him a new car. He was absolutely ecstatic and promised to pray for my good fortune in the years to come.

On the 5th January 1947, we took off on the short flight to RAF Mauripur, Karachi. Normally all planes flying in and out of India called at Karachi. We spent the night at Karachi and set out early next morning for Basra, in Iraq. As we flew along the coast of Baluchistan towards the Persian Gulf, I noticed streaks of oil running along the starboard outer engine. Although each engine carried 35 gallons of lubricating oil, it was difficult to gauge the rate of loss, so I advised the Pilot to make an emergency landing at RAF Sharjah, an emergency airfield, at the mouth of the Gulf, in the Trucial Arab States. This was accepted without question and at the end of a three-hour flight we landed at Sharjah. Apart from the weekly Dakota, bringing supplies, visits from aircraft were a rare occurrence and the whole station turned out to greet us. "We've got an oil leak," I announced. "Never mind the oil leak," was the response, "open the bar!" They were all set to have an instant party, but we had no wish to spend the night there and that is what too many drinks would have meant. We persuaded them to despatch a couple of mechanics to the aircraft and they soon found that a loose union was the cause of the oil leak. They tightened it, we said our farewells, and took off for Basra.

INDIA REVISITED

A further three hours later, we landed in darkness at RAF Shaibah, near Basra. By the time we settled in, it was late. With an early start in the morning, we decided to go straight to bed. I found out some months later that, had I visited the Sergeant's Mess, I would have most certainly met my old friend Paddy Curtis and that would just as certainly have meant flying the next day with a hangover. The next day was a long one, with a four and a half hour trip to RAF Almaza, in Egypt, and then on to RAF Luqa, Malta, a five and a quarter hour flight.

In spite of the long day we all had enough energy to visit Valletta and to savour the delights of 'The Street Named Straight,' colloquially known as 'The Gut.' This was where all the bars were located with their 'hostesses.' These girls were employed by the bar keepers to persuade their customers to buy them drinks. The drinks were always green and we suspected, were just coloured water for which they charged an exorbitant price. As we walked down the street the barmen would stand at the doors calling out, "Hay, Blue boys, come inside, we got what you want." Eventually I ended up in a half empty bar with a single hostess who looked as though she had seen better days. We were in earnest conversation when a bearded sailor sat himself down and took over. The hostess then turned her attention to the sailor. I left and returned to camp. The next day, as we winged our way towards the south of France, I thought to myself, "When you're heading for disaster, you can always count on the Navy for rescue."

As we approached the French coast, Doug Manton our Wireless Operator, reported he had received instruction that due to adverse weather conditions in the UK, we were to land at a French Air Force base near Bordeaux. We had a Group Captain onboard who could speak fluent French and he came in useful as soon as we landed. He obtained from the French ground crew a ladder so that I could get onto the wing and carry out a few checks in preparation for the morrow's anticipated flight. That night we all went to a nightclub in Bordeaux including our high-ranking passengers. Then, as now, very little English was spoken in France and I found myself dancing with a French girl who could speak no English. I was equally ill-versed in French and so each time she said anything I would reply, "Excusez-moi." I would then leave her standing on the dance floor while I dashed over to the Group Captain for a translation. I would then ask him for the French for my reply and dash back and deliver it to my dancing partner. She was quite amused by the whole thing and really entered into the spirit of it.

The next morning we took off for home and landed some three hours later at RAF Manston, in Kent. After a brief stop for instructions we continued to the English Electric Aircraft Company's airfield at Burton Wood, in Lancashire, where we said farewell to our Lancastrian. The crew also went their separate ways. Doug Manton and I, the two non-commissioned Officers in the crew, went straight down to London where we spent the night in 'The Regent Palace Hotel,' just off Piccadilly. The next morning we reported to the Air Ministry where, after a brief interview, we were sent on two weeks disembarkation leave and told to look out for telegraphed instructions regarding our next postings.

9
BRIZE NORTON

About half way through my disembarkation leave I received a telegram from the Air Ministry stating that, on completion of my leave, I was to precede to 4 Group Head Quarters, at York, now the site of York University. After spending the night in transit accommodation at York I had a very pleasant interview the next morning with an Officer whose job it was to 'fit me in somewhere.' We started by looking at a large wall map of Great Britain. "Where do you live?" he asked. "Birmingham," I replied, "but I don't want to be a week-day airman, anywhere is fine, so long as it's in the south where the weather's warmer." "How about Brize Norton?" he asked after scanning the south of the country. "Where's that?" I enquired. "Roughly between Oxford and Cheltenham," was his reply. "That's OK," I said. "Only one snag, though," he continued, "the unit is T.C.D.U. that stands for Transport Command Development Unit. The CO is Wing Commander Scragg and he won't accept anyone until he's interviewed and approved them. You should be alright though he's an ex Halton boy and so are you." With that the interview was closed and I was on my way. The train journey took me through Birmingham and so, with permission, I spent the weekend at home.

It was the last week of January 1947, and over the weekend it started snowing. My first view of RAF Brize Norton was a snow scene and this remained the scene for the next ten weeks. For most of this time the temperature was below zero. It was the coldest winter for a hundred years. Every few days it would snow and by the time the thaw came in April, the accumulation of snow was so great, that it resulted in some of the worst floods in living memory.

The day after I arrived on the camp I had the interview with the CO, W/Cdr. Scragg, of which I had been forewarned. The first thing that I noticed as I entered his office was a large notice on his wall which proclaimed, "The difficult, we do immediately. The impossible takes a little longer." Since then I have seen this on many occasions but this was my first introduction. I soon realised that here was a 'super-efficient perfectionist.' To look at he had the figure and the walk of the film star, John Wayne, though not the features. Some time later somebody produced a 1938 copy of the magazine, 'Flight,' which featured an illustrated article of the annual Hendon Air Show with a fly-past by three biplanes. The leader was Douglas Bader, the famous leg-less Pilot, though at that time he was not legless. One of the wingmen was 'Flight Sergeant Scragg,' who had changed little in appearance in the ensuing nine years. My interview with him did not last very long. He asked me a few questions about my background and then welcomed me to the unit.

There was little or no flying during the adverse weather. At the same time there was a severe shortage of all types of fuel. The war had plunged the nation deeply into debt and the cry was, "Export or die." Hence, most of the coal that was produced was exported, and oil cost dollars of which the country had pitiably few. Most of the schools were closed as were a number of the less important RAF stations. When I went home on leave I would go down to the gas works and stand in a long queue for a relatively small bag of coke to augment the family's meagre supply of coal. On the camp I complained to the CO that the bath water was too cold to bathe in. Typically, W/Cdr. Scragg said, "Draw a thermometer out of stores and take the water temperature twice a day for a week. Then bring me the figures. I'll take it up with the clerk-of-works." A couple of days after I handed him the figures the water temperature rose miraculously.

The Government Minister of Fuel and Power during the big freeze was Emanuel Shinwell. At the next cabinet reshuffle he was appointed War Minister. This gave rise to the popular joke, "When he was Minister of Fuel, there was no fuel. Now that he's Minister of War, hopefully there'll be no war."

The nation had become so used to rationing during the war that the government decided that they could use rationing as a tool to service the enormous national debt that the war had created. Before the war 60% of the nation's food was imported and though much was done during the war to redress this, relatively little of our food remained home grown. Eventually the rationing became so severe that when the meat ration was reduced to ten pence worth per week, many housewives took to the streets in protest.

At Brize Norton, I was confronted with two unfamiliar aircraft, the Halifax and the York. The Halifax was a transport version of the famous bomber that had so ably supported the Lancasters bombing Germany during the war. It was used mainly for glider towing, dropping paratroops, through a large hatch in the floor at the rear of the aircraft, and for dropping a large pannier, held in the bomb compartment, containing a field-gun and a jeep. The York was built by Avro, the manufacturers of the Lancaster. It was a four engined, high winged aircraft, with the engines, main plane, wheels and tail plane of the Lancaster except that it had a third central stabilising fin. The fuselage was a new design consisting of a square sectioned, wide bodied, open space with the crew positioned in the very front. It was designed for a crew of four, two Pilots, a Navigator and a Wireless Operator. The Flight Engineer was the second Pilot. We also had on the unit a number of the ubiquitous Dakotas, including one of the 'glider snatching' variety, with the winch and accoutrements, that I had managed to escape from, two years before. To operate it there were two Winch Operators who were ex Flight Engineers, Percy Pearce and Iva Maldoom. In due course I found I had a lot in common with Iva, who we always called Mall, and eventually, when I graduated to a small room, known as a bunk, adjacent to the barrack room, I shared this with him.

On my departure to India the year before, I had virtually severed all links with my wartime-adopted family, the Curtis's. Amongst them, my affair with Rene was common knowledge and I had slipped, somewhat, in their popularity ratings. My mother, however, knew nothing of it and kept asking me to go down and recover some article that she had, unintentionally, left with them when my family moved from their temporary accommodation in Torquay to Birmingham. For a couple of months I had used the weather as an excuse for procrastinating but when the bleak winter finally released its grip, I had no option but to take my courage in both hands and journey down to Torquay. I travelled overnight and dead on nine o'clock in the morning I called at the Inland Revenue offices where Paddy's father had worked when I was last in touch. I was told that he, along with his wife, were now steward and stewardess of a club in the town, and so thither I made my way. To my stunned surprise, the door was opened by Rene and she was just as amazed to see me. She quickly regained her composure and invited me in where a further surprise awaited me. I had been completely forgiven for my misdeeds and was welcomed like a prodigal son.

Even with me out of sight and out of mind, Rene and her husband, John, were having difficulty in adjusting to post war married life. Rene was care-taking her parent's house in Torquay while John was in Germany, a member of the CCG (Control Commission of Germany). This was the organisation, staffed mostly by ex servicemen, which 'governed' the British Sector of Germany. Almost unintentionally our affair restarted and on my return to Brize Norton, we were again in touch. I returned the article to my mother who to the best of my knowledge never found out about my problems with the Curtis family. Her outlook was rather Victorian and had she known, it is doubtful whether she would have been as accommodating as they were.

It was about this time that my records had returned from India resulting in two rather pleasant developments. Firstly I received a lump sum in back pay for the time that I had spent in India. The Air Ministry had somehow lost track of me. They even sent a telegram to my home in Birmingham telling me that I was posted to No. 1 Ferry Unity, at Pershore. When my mother returned it with the information that I was in India, they started to track me down. However it took the whole nine months that I was there before my records arrived by when we were returning to the UK and my records took a further four months to catch up with me. All this time I was being paid on an impress account. I never did find out exactly what this was but it seemed to work rather like an emergency tax code, when maximum tax is levied until all the details are known, when a final settlement is made. Of course in the case of the impress account, in place of maximum tax levied, it was minimum sum paid.

A further pleasant surprise came from my Mother. For the last four or five years I had been making her a cash allotment, from my pay, of half a crown a week (13p) I

BRIZE NORTON

was not sure what it was for, except that it made me feel like a provider. My mother had decided to save it for me and now thought it time to present me with these savings of around thirty pounds, a very useful sum in those days. Finally my 'Bounty Scheme' application had succeeded. I was presented with £25, demobilised and remobilised in the same day, and despatched to the 'demob.' Centre near Blackpool to be fitted out with a civilian suit. With all this money, my thoughts turned to a car. However, to buy a new car one had to have ones name on a waiting list for two or three years and consequently second hand cars, even those ready for the scrap heap, cost almost as much as new ones. My cousin, Frank, had a civilian job in Birmingham and was living at home. He had a certain amount of money that had been left to him on the death of his Mother, some years before. Between us we had enough to buy a 'Hillman Minx.' The Hillman was our choice because the RAF used them extensively and we reasoned, spare parts would have been manufactured and would be readily available.

After a brief search, we tracked one down in Birmingham which we bought for £300. We soon found that there were a host of things wrong with it but our first priority was to get it to Brize Norton where I could work on it in the evenings. I had arranged to pick up a colleague on weekend leave in Birmingham and we set off at around seven o'clock on the Monday morning. We got as far as Stoe-in-the-Wold when we came to a halt with a flat battery. The generator wasn't charging. We waited until eight o'clock when the local garage opened and had the battery boost charged for half an hour.

We then continued as far as Burford. The main street in Burford has a fairly steep hill to climb. We could not climb it because the clutch was slipping badly. Ever resourceful, and knowing that reverse gear was the lowest of all the gears, and therefore least demanding on the clutch, I turned the car round and successfully reversed up the hill. When my colleague recounted this at the camp I had my leg pulled unmercifully.

I worked assiduously on the car but progress was slow. There was so much wrong with it. One day I drove it a few miles to the Royal Naval School of Music. We were to play rugby against them. I had taken the car because I was on duty later and could not stop for the main purpose of all coarse rugby matches, the booze-up after the match. The clerk-of-works, a man in his forties, came with the team and also had to return early. He was sat in the back of the car when we went over a hump-backed bridge at speed. I watched in alarm through the rear view mirror as he rose in the air, hit his head on the roof, bounced down on the seat and rose half way to the roof again. It was then that I realised that the rear shock absorbers were not working. I did apologise but he seemed too dazed to appreciate my concern.

There was one more major fault with the car. The bush on the steering arm was so badly worn that one could turn the steering wheel half a turn in either direction without anything happening. I was beginning to get despondent thinking that I would have to spend the price of the car again on spare parts, when I received an offer I couldn't refuse. Flight Lieutenant

BRIZE NORTON

Pearce, one of the Pilots, had a 1936 model 'Ford Popular' which wasn't good enough for his wife. It was good enough for me, though, because everything worked. We finally did a deal whereby he would take the Hillman with all the outstanding work needed on it in exchange for the Ford and a cash payment to me. This allowed me to pay Frank back his half of the investment, as the shared idea wasn't going to work. It also gave me a car that I could drive and not just work on.

At that time, the meagre petrol ration, for private motoring, was abolished. No private mileage was allowed except for essential journeys like travelling between bases either on transfer or temporary duty. All petrol for commercial vehicles had a special die introduced which could be detected at the exhaust. It was a criminal offence to use commercial petrol in a private vehicle. However, in the world of the RAF it was a different ball game. Here there were two kinds of petrol for aircraft. Hundred Octane for the supercharged engines and 73 octane for the normally aspirated engines as fitted in the Austers and other small planes. There was a general belief that 100-octane fuel burnt a car's exhaust valves out and so the acquisition of this fuel was never regarded with any suspicion. The 73 octane, on the other hand, was regarded as dynamite which everyone kept well clear of.

Having studied fuel technology on the Flight Engineers course, I had an advantage. The octane value of a fuel was merely a measure of its resistance to detonation expressed as a percentage against two fuels, Heptane at 0 and iso-octane at 100. The high-octane values were achieved by the addition of Tetraethyl Lead. 100 octane was introduced with the supercharging of aero engines to prevent detonation. At the same time the additional heat generated by superchargers could burn out exhaust valves which were then filled with sodium for cooling. In the mind of the general public, the exhaust valve problem was associated with the fuel rather than the supercharging. The supercharger was the real culprit. I did my best to keep this misconception going as 100-octane aircraft fuel was freely available for cleaning and other such purposes.

After the worst winter for a hundred years the summer that followed was the best many people could remember. The hot, sunny days seemed endless and we spent many hours swimming in the upper reaches of the Thames. I had become friendly with a redundant Flight Engineer named Frank Sanders. He had been shot down in 1943 but had managed to evade capture and made contact with the French Resistance. Unfortunately he, along with others, had been betrayed to the Germans who swooped on them in a Paris street. Frank was imprisoned and told that, as he was in civilian clothes, he would be shot as a spy. He spent a month under sentence of death during which time his whole head of hair turned white. Eventually, instead of being shot, he was sent to a prisoner of war camp from which he made two unsuccessful attempts to escape. For his exploits he was awarded the MBE on his return home. At Brize Norton we had a number of German Prisoners of War awaiting repatriation and doing menial jobs on the camp. Frank used to delight in taunting them. He would bark an order at them, in German, like "Arbeiten" (Work!). The prisoner would look at him with a nervous smile, unsure whether or not he was joking. Then Frank would laugh and we would all join in the joke, even the prisoner, though with less mirth than us.

When repatriated, Frank received all his back pay for the time that he was a prisoner, several hundred pounds, with which he bought a Ford Prefect car in much better condition than my Hillman. He and I decided to go camping in Cornwall. We both managed to get three weeks leave, borrowed a 14 ft. 'ridge' tent from the Army, and cadged a fair amount of illicit rations from the buxom WAAF Sergeant in charge of the cookhouse. Being totally inexperienced campers we knew nothing of campsites and generally approached farmers for permission to camp in their fields. This we invariably got. Our first pitch was in Falmouth which, though it was beautiful, lacked any social life. We therefore struck camp and headed for Newquay. Here we found a farmer's field about three miles out of Newquay, a town that we visited nightly. Unfortunately the farmer had neglected to tell us that there were cows in the field and the cows seemed keen to share our comforts. To keep them out we had to lace up the tent which resulted in us over-sleeping and shortening our days of adventure. To solve this problem we had breakfast before we went to bed at night so that we were able to get up, dress and go straight out in the morning. This was probably when I acquired a taste for porridge for supper.

Back at Brize Norton Frank and I, along with a dozen or

more Sergeants, occupied a single large barrack room. Many of the occupants were married with homes in the midlands or southern England. They would go home every weekend. Among those of us who's hearts and minds were in the RAF, there was a technical Sergeant, an ex Halton boy, whose surname was Clerk. So inevitably he was called 'Nobby.' Nobby Clerk had a wicked sense of humour and a hilarious turn of phrase. Among the weekend boys was a short, rather portly, Sergeant who at one time had been stationed at RAF Henlow, in Bedfordshire, where he had met and married a girl from nearby Biggleswade where she still lived. Every Friday evening he would get himself ready, in a state of great anticipation, to dash off on weekend leave. Nobby would lie on his side, on top of his bed, his elbow on the pillow and his head cupped in his open palm and would declare, in a loud drawl, "There'll be screams of delight in Biggleswade tonight." He always referred to the sex act as a 'laminated session' as one was on top of the other. At the time Frank Sanders had a girlfriend in Cheltenham who he used to see every Saturday night. She was engaged to a boy who lived in another part of the country. The day before her wedding, Frank was getting ready to go and see her for the last time. Nobby, in his usual relaxed posture, asked him, "What's her husband going to say when he finds out that someone's been there before him?" "Oh he won't notice," replied Frank. "What," exclaimed Nobby, staring at Frank's pelvis, "After sliding up and down that for six months?"

All through the summer, my affair with Rene was a bit on, off. Early on she had come up to the camp for a few days in a bed & breakfast. Now my feelings were changing. My thoughts were turning to younger women. As we did not seem to have any future I felt it unfair to act any longer as a stumbling block to her reconciliation with her husband. I therefore resolved to have a 'heart to heart', 'cards on the table' session with her and to this end, I arranged to meet her in Reading on a Friday evening. We went a few miles up river to a couple of adjacent picturesque little villages called Goring and Streatley, where we booked into a hotel. It was a beautiful setting and it would have been a most romantic weekend if the purpose had been different. Eventually we talked the subject out and Rene reluctantly agreed to return to the situation as it was the previous year when we were out of contact. On Monday morning we walked over to the main road and waited. Eventually a colleague returning from weekend leave on his motorcycle, picked me up, as arranged. As we drove off, with me on the pillion seat, I turned and waved goodbye and that was the last time I ever saw her.

Twenty-five years later, as a sales manager for Chubb Fire, I called in at a country pub, in the dark, at a road junction near Street, in Somerset, to ask directions. I was amazed to find that the landlady was Rene's cousin, Betty, whose mother used to work in the 'Duke of York' in St. John's Wood, during the war. Betty told me that John and Rene had eventually got their act together and had raised two strapping lads. "All's well that ends well," I thought. - To help salve my conscience.

About a week after this fateful weekend, we set off on our first long haul overseas trip. We were testing a piece of new radar technology known as 'Cloud and Collision Warning' which was intended to detect the dangerous Cumulus Nimbus clouds. We were told that the Cu. Nims. at Singapore were bigger and better than in the UK and that is where and why we were going. We wouldn't argue with that but we suspected that the real reason was to give ourselves a break from the austerity at home. We flew out in a 'York'. The journey took us six days with night stops at the following RAF stations. Luqa (Malta), Fayid (Suez Canal), Habaniyah (Baghdad), Mauripur (Karachi), Negombo (Colombo) and finally Changi (Singapore).

On the way complaints were heard that the toilet at the rear of the fuselage stank. So almost as soon as we landed at Singapore, W/Cdr. Scragg turned to me and said, "See if you can put some ventilation in the loo, Engineer". I went straight to the station workshops and drew out of the stores a sandbag and a mallet. The sandbag consisted of a green, heavy canvas cushion about a foot square filled with sand. The mallet had one of its striking surfaces rounded to a half sphere. Other than the ex Halton boys, few RAF technicians would have known what the sand bags were for though every workshop stores had them. Fewer still would have ever seen one in use. Consequently when word got round that one had been drawn out of the stores and was in use in the 'metal bashing room,' a small crowd gathered round to watch. I placed a piece of aluminium sheet, about the same size as the sand bag, on top of the bag and began beating it with the rounded end of the mallet until it formed a streamlined shape with an open end and a flange all round the enclosed area. I took this to the aircraft, cut a 2-inch hole in the outer skin of the loo and riveted my 'master piece' over the hole. The idea was that the depression at the open end would suck air out of the loo. It seemed to work for there were no further complaints.

We spent almost three weeks in Singapore flying towards Cu. Nim. clouds to test and calibrate the radar. One of these flights took us over Sumatra where we crossed the equator. Before the war 'crossing the line,' as it was called, invariably on a ship, was such a rare occurrence that it merited a ceremony involving someone dressed as 'Neptune' and many high jinks after which a certificate was issued to everybody. Later Jet travel made the crossing an every-day affair and the practice died out. But at this time, elements of it still lingered and although there was no ceremony, we were all issued with a joke certificate entitled 'Shooting the Line' (instead of crossing it). Today the return flight would take a mere 13 hours.

On another overseas trip, we were heading for Malta as dusk was approaching. I noticed that the generator voltage was creeping up and decided that the Carbon-Pile voltage regulators were getting too warm. To cool them, by allowing air to circulate round them, I was removing the metal panel behind which they were housed, when it slipped out of my hands and fell across the exposed battery terminals directly below. There was a loud bang and a flash as the battery split and the acid started to leak onto the floor. By the time we landed it was quite dark and as soon as the engines were cut we were plunged into darkness. We had already signalled our plight ahead and as soon as we came to a final halt the ground crew were on board with neutralising alkali to mop the floor and replace the batteries. I was glad we were not flying with W/Cdr. Scragg.

Flying with W/Cdr. Scragg as Captain could be quite stressful. He had a habit of browsing through obscure technical publications and questioning his crew members on what he had read. On one occasion on which I flew with him, while we were doing the external, pre-flight checks, he asked me a highly technical question about the Pito Head Heater. The Pito head was an appendage that measured the speed of airflow and therefore the speed of the plane. It required a heater to prevent it from icing up. I did not know the answer to his question but he said nothing. He just looked at me disdainfully as if I was some sort of oaf. When I returned to the Flight Engineer's office the Engineer Leader, F/Lt. Britain, pounced on me saying, "What did he ask you? What did he ask you?" When I told him he immediately started raking through our technical publications for the answer in case he was asked the same question.

On another occasion I flew with the CO in a Halifax to RAF Dishforth, in Yorkshire. We returned in the early evening. When we got out of the plane he said, "Half an hour to get something to eat and then back again for night circuits and bumps." Knowing him as we did, half an hour meant half an hour. The servicing Sergeant asked me if the plane needed refuelling. I made a very hurried calculation and wanting to avoid any delay that would spell trouble, I said, "no." Dead on the half hour we were back at the aircraft ready to fly. As the engines started a quick glance at the fuel gauges told me that I had made a mistake and that we were going to be short. "Never mind," I thought, "These old Halifaxs are always developing minor faults. Let's hope something goes wrong soon." As we took off and landed, took off and landed, I kept looking at the fuel gauges as the hands moved inexorably towards the danger marks. The Signals leader, standing by the gauges with nothing better to do, also started looking at them. "How much fuel have we got left, Engineer?" he asked over the intercom. "Why doesn't he keep his big mouth shut," I thought, but answered, "We are a little short." "What's that?" asked the CO as we taxied round for the next take off. "Have we got enough for another circuit, Engineer?" "Oh yes," I replied. "Then we'll do one," he said and continued taxiing. We stopped at the end of the runway. "What's wrong with the flaps, Engineer?" the CO asked. "Oh God," I thought, "it's here at last, but too late to save me." "There's a fault on the selector, sir," I said, "It'll have to go back to Servicing." Reluctantly he turned round and taxied back. When we got out of the aircraft he said to the Sergeant in charge of servicing and also to me, "In the office, both of you." He had me standing outside the door while he interrogated the Sergeant. Then he had us change places to hear my version. I told him exactly what had happened and why I had declined the request for refuelling. He gave me a short, sharp lecture on safety which I didn't really need and concluded, "You haven't heard the last of this, I'll see you in the morning." In fact he never said a word about it again.

His last remark was probably meant to make sure I had a bad night to reinforce his message about safety.

We returned to the Sergeant's Mess where a party was in full swing. Every week the mess would have an open night, when a coach would pick up, and later return, a number of girls from Oxford, Whitney and surrounding areas. This included some nurses from 'Freelands,' a local nursing home. My current girlfriend was one of these nurses and as I had missed most of the evening, she and her friend and her friend's male escort, all agreed that I would take them home in my car rather than go on the coach. On the return trip, with only my colleague and me in the car, we came to a sudden halt on the far side of the airfield. I soon established that we had run out of petrol and so we pushed the car off the road and started walking the 3 miles or so back to our billets. As we walked cheerfully along I turned to my companion and said, "There's one thing about it, there's not many people could boast of running out of petrol twice in the same night."

Apart from the good social life sport was a major item on the Brize Norton itinerary. Wednesday afternoon was devoted to the sport of one's choice. My choice was rugby and every Wednesday we played another service team either at home or away. One week we played against the Police Training School at Eynsham Hall. After the match we found that they had the same sort of social arrangement as we did with mostly the same girls in attendance. It was quite a party. On Saturdays most of the rugby players who did not go home for the weekend would play for Whitney Rugby Club. We always felt that the purpose of the game was to work up a thirst for the beer session after.

As members of Whitney Rugby Club we were entitled to 'Players Tickets' which gave us entry to the International Rugby matches at Twickenham when England was playing at home. On the grass between the side stands and the touch line there were several rows of forms, or benches, which were reserved for those with 'Player's Tickets.' One of my fellow rugby players was a Cornishman named Geoff Lavin who had been to school with the current England Rugby Captain. He used to say, "When we were at school he was just Johnny Carpenter. When he went to Oxford he became John Kendal-Carpenter."

On one occasion Geoff and I were at Twickenham, seated on a 'player's bench' near the tunnel. All around us were young men encouraging the players by using their first names. At the end of the match as the teams were going into the tunnel Geoff called out, "Well done John." The England Captain, recognizing Geoff's voice, looked over and replied, "Hello Geoff." Those around us looked at Geoff with amazement, as if to say, "Who is this person on first name terms with the England Captain?

When the Rugby Season was over we would turn to other sports, which soon led me to the gym. Unfortunately, after finding a pair of boxing gloves one day, the PTI (Physical Training Instructor) spotted me and said, "Just the man I've been looking for. We've had a lad, a novice like you, who's volunteered to take part in the forthcoming boxing tournament. You're just the person to match him with." The person he named was a technical Warrant Officer with whom I was on friendly terms. He had made a remarkable recovery from the state that he had been in as a Japanese prisoner of war. I liked him a lot and at first was reluctant to fight him. He reassured me however that it was only for fun and on the night we both entered into the spirit of the thing by lounging around in the dressing area whilst the serious boxers were busy shadow boxing, jumping and waving their arms in the air. At one stage of our contest I had the advantage of him but, remembering my state of unfitness, I desisted from exploiting it. Thus I lost the initiative and with it, the contest. I was later glad of this as he went on to represent the station against a boxing club where he was almost certainly outclassed.

Although we enjoyed much of the fun side of life we also had discipline to contend with and some of us tried to combine the two. Most weeks there was CO's parade. We all had to form up on the parade ground in squads, or flights as they were called in the RAF. At one stage in the proceedings, the Padre would come on and lead us in prayer. Before he did, however, the SWO (Station Warrant Officer, the equivalent of the Army's Sergeant Major) would bawl out, "Fall out the Roman Catholics and Jews." With that, our little group would walk off the parade ground. Nobody ever asked us if we were Roman Catholics or Jews or anything else for that matter, and it gave us a break from the monotony of the parade.

When there were no prayers we would go into our fainting act. In this the 'fainter' would position himself directly in front of the 'catcher.' At a given signal the 'fainter,' standing rigidly at attention, would start to fall backwards while the 'catcher' took a step forward, caught him and dragged him, feet trailing, off the parade ground and onto the grassy knoll beside the barrack block. At the first opportunity we would disappear and return to the Sergeant's Mess. At the official level there seemed to be a peculiar indifference to the physical well being of the troops. One day a notice appeared on the notice board, under the heading, P.O.R.s (Periodical Occurrence Reports). One of the Sergeants had died of a fatal illness. The notice displayed his number, rank and name, and his obituary read, "Deceased. - Struck off the Ration Strength."

Once a year, every RAF station was inspected by the AOC (Air Officer Commanding). This was a big occasion, and not dissimilar to a visit by the queen. Everything had to be scrubbed and polished. If it moved, it was saluted, if it didn't, it was painted. AOC's parade was like a command performance. It was rehearsed several times before the big day. At one such rehearsal, with band present, the SWO walked onto the parade ground and shouted, "March on." Spontaneously several of the NCO aircrew flight broke into subdued singing, "Marchons, Marchons," from the French National Anthem. They were cut short when the band opened up with the 'Col. Bogey' march, so they changed to "Bollocks, and the same to you." We had words to the next march also. "Have you ever caught your bollocks in a rat trap? A rat trap?" By now the flight was in a really giggly mood and Flt.Lt. Fitzgerald, who was in charge of the Officer Aircrew Flight, compounded this. Flt.Lt. Fitzgerald was a Flight Engineer but always seemed a little bit slow on the uptake. One day, in the Engineers' office, to pull his leg, I asked him, "Eh Fitz, how do you spell Phillips? Is it Filips?" "Two Ls," he replied emphatically and wondered why every one in the room laughed. When Fitz marched his flight onto the parade ground he gave his command, "Flight, attention! – I mean Halt!" This really got us going, and by the end of the parade, as we marched past the Station Commander with "Eyes Right," the CO shouted back, "Halt that flight." He walked up to Green, my motorcycling friend, and said, "What's the joke lad come on let's share it." What are you laughing at?" Green normally had the most sombre face and when he answered, "It's my natural expression sir," I thought, "It's going to be me next." I was literally shaking with laughter but determined to keep a straight face. If I'd been challenged I was ready to say, "I've got the ague, sir."

In the spring of 1948, I was sent on a 'Survival and Rescue course' to RAF Thorny Island, between Hayling Island and Chichester, on the English South Coast. It was a very enjoyable experience for after some brief lectures, mostly on the art of sailing, we took to the sea. The class was split in two, half going out to sea in a high speed Air/Sea Rescue Launch, with rubber dinghies and the other half, going up in an Anson aircraft to see what people in a dinghy looked like from the air. Later the two halves would swap over. We went into the dinghies first. We had two dinghies on board, a large one that could contain eight men, and a small, fighter Pilots' dinghy, barely big enough for one person. I volunteered to go in the small one and as soon as I was safely ensconced in it the launch turned and headed away at speed. This was meant to be a joke to make me panic but I was more concerned with the discomfort of sitting in the icy cold sea water that had lapped over the shallow sides of the dinghy and soaked my thick serge battle dress trousers. When our turn came to view the scene from the air, I was amazed at how difficult it was to spot, even the largest dinghy, from less than 1,000 ft.

Following this and the lectures on sailing, we took to the 'Airborne Lifeboats.' These were whaler type boats, about 20 ft. long, with a large, inflatable buoyancy chamber fore and aft beneath which were storage areas in the sharply pointed bow and stern of the vessel. They had masts, sails and an Austin Marine auxiliary engine with fuel to drive them for 600 miles. They were called 'Airborne Lifeboats' because they were carried in the bomb compartment of rescue aircraft and dropped by parachute to airmen cast adrift in a dinghy. There were three boats and the class was divided into three with some six or seven 'hands' in each boat. Three 'Captains' were selected from the few in the class who claimed to have had sailing experience. As soon as we had found our sea legs we set sail for the Isle of White.

Our Captain was an intensely serious lad devoid of anything resembling a sense of humour and giving no indication that he could subscribe to our axiom that 'Life was a game that should be played with a smiling face.' Consequently, when three of us were crouched beneath the buoyancy chamber, whispering, he asked us what we were doing. We replied, "Plotting a mutiny." At first he ignored us but when we rose with shouts of, "Get him boys, tie him to the mast!" and proceeded to do so. He remonstrated so violently, and even shouted for help from the other boats, that we agreed that he was never going to enter into the spirit of the thing. We therefore decided to abandon him and just proceeded to enjoy the sunshine and fresh air though it was a bit chilly.

For our social life in the evenings, we would frequently go into Chichester, the local town, about 10 miles away. On one such visit I met an Australian nurse from the local hospital. We were getting on so well that I decided to take a chance and let her in on the fact that I had missed the last bus back to camp, in the hope that I would win her hospitality. When she said she would find me a bed for the night in the hospital I was convinced that I had scored. However, she was nothing if not accurate in her statement. She took me to a disused ward where she pulled a bed from among a collection in one corner. Having made it up with bedclothes and after promising to return to get me out of the hospital in the morning, she disappeared for the night. As good as her word she was there early the next morning, in her uniform hustling me along. As we crept down a corridor we turned a corner and to our horror there, in front of us, and bearing down on us, was the Hospital Matron with her entourage. The nurse and I, both stopped, turned, and ran in different directions to 'confuse the enemy.' I found my own way out of the hospital and back to camp. Though I visited Chichester again on a few occasions I never saw the girl again. She was probably being kept in as a punishment.

If our lives seemed to be preoccupied with girls and sex it was because our thoughts were. Frank Sanders used to say that in the prisoner-of-war camps they had a saying, "Belly empty, subject food. Belly full, subject sex," It was with this thought in mind that many years later I coined one of my personal 'Pearls,' "The best aphrodisiac is a cocktail of healthy youth, boredom and a full stomach."

The course lasted a month altogether and on my return to Brize Norton, I was officially appointed, 'Survival and Rescue Officer.' One of my functions was to give lectures and show films to all the aircrew. From the command library I sent for three main films. 'Land and Live in the Arctic,' 'Land and Live in the Desert' and 'Land and Live in the Jungle.' These were excellent films, made in Hollywood and featuring Van Heflin, a Hollywood star. Whenever we had a film show W/Cdr. Scragg, the CO, would sit in on it. Then, because he was always under pressure, he would get up and leave. As soon as his back was turned there was a general cry from the audience, "Show them backwards, show them backwards." I would then reverse the projector and as we watched men abscaling up cliffs, rising into the air on folding parachutes, and disappearing into aeroplanes that were flying backwards, peels of laughter could be heard outside the auditorium. I had to keep peeping out of the door to make sure the CO was not about. He would have had 'my guts for garters,' as the saying went.

When I eventually graduated to a bunk, a little two-bedded room just off the main barrack room, which I shared with Mall, I got involved in the world of 'Nylon Rug Making.' Mall was one of the two 'Winch Operators' connected with the 'Glider Snatching' operation described in Chapter 7. This operation utilised a nylon rope because nylon gave it a certain amount of elasticity. Each rope had a limited life which was restricted to some half dozen snatches after which it was scrapped. Mall and Percy, the other Winch Operator, would unwind these ropes, cut strands of it into short lengths, and using a special tool which they had made themselves, they would weave them into a piece of Hessian to make a rug. White rugs were not everybody's choice but at that time there were no nylon dies. We found that soaking the nylon in Potassium Permanganate (Condy's Fluid) would turn it a golden colour so we announced that rugs were available in any colour so long as they were white or golden. I made a semicircular, golden hearthrug, about a metre in diameter, which I presented to my mother. She put it down but I was never sure that she didn't take it up again when I wasn't there.

I was always keen to enjoy any new experience. One day a notice appeared on D.R.O.s (Daily Routine Orders) inviting any one who wished to volunteer to do a parachute-jumping course at RAF Upper Heyford. The idea appealed to me but I didn't fancy going on my own. I approached a friend and asked him if he would join me. His answer was, "No I'm a patient sort of guy, I can wait until the aeroplane lands." In the end it proved to be a missed experience that I regretted all my life. This incident prompted me in later life to coin another of my 'Pearls,' "When looking back on my life, the only experiences I regret are the ones that I missed." To this I later added, "Every experience has enriched my life, even the bad ones."

10
THE BERLIN AIR LIFT

On the conclusion of World War II in Europe in 1945, the victorious allies occupied Germany by dividing the country into areas of responsibility. These were called 'Zones.' The British Zone was North West Germany, the American Zone was Southern Germany and the Soviet Zone was Eastern Germany. The French also had a small zone on their border, not because they were in any way denigrated but, having been occupied themselves for the previous five years, they lacked the armed forces necessary to police a large area. Germany's capital, Berlin, fell within the Soviet Zone and it was divided into three sectors known as the British, American and Soviet Sectors. Access to their sectors from their respective Zones was given to the British and Americans by treaty. There were specified rail and road links through the Soviet Zone along with Air Corridors.

In the summer of 1948, Joseph Stalin, the Soviet dictator,

and considered by some to be even more despotic than Hitler, threw down the gauntlet to the British and Americans. Unilaterally and arbitrarily he closed the surface links between West Germany and Berlin. To also blockade the air corridors would have involved shooting down aircraft which would have meant the start of World War III and at that time the Americans had the Atomic Bomb and the Soviets did not. The western allies therefore decided to supply West Berlin by air and to this end they set up a massive air lift which continued for over a year and became known as 'The Berlin Airlift.'

At the start the whole of Transport Command was deployed on this operation. The large four engined, load carrying, York aircraft were based in West Germany to fly into Berlin. The smaller Dakotas were used to shuttle between Britain and West Germany with supplies for the York bases. We, the Transport Command Development Unit, had one York and it was immediately dispatched, with a crew of four, to the ex. Luftwaffe airfield at Wunstorf, near Hanover. I was the Flight Engineer and second Pilot and the Captain was our flight commander, Flt.Lt. Max Chivers. Max was a true Londoner and never pretended to be anything else. He was a complete extrovert and was universally popular. He would never stand on ceremony and would often call me 'Dead Head.' I never resented this, in fact I regarded it as a term of endearment. I reasoned that, if he really thought that I was a 'dead head,' he would not have continually asked me to fly with him. The other two members of the crew were the Navigator, a Flight Lieutenant, and the Wireless Operator, a Warrant Officer

THE BERLIN AIR LIFT

like me, named Jones. He was always addressed as 'Jonah.'

On the 18th of July we set off for RAF Dishforth, in Yorkshire to pick up a cargo. The next day we flew to RAF Lyneham, in Wiltshire, to clear customs, and then straight to RAF Gatow in the British sector of Berlin. From there to our German base at Wunstorf where we settled in. We found the system highly organised and well established, with planes taking off and landing every few minutes round the clock. Each crew was expected to do twelve hours on with thirteen hours off. Each twelve-hour shift would involve three round trips to Berlin and the extra hour off duty would ensure an even share of night flying for all. If the plane, or the crew, were not fully ready to go at the appointed time the trip was cancelled and both would have to wait four hours for their next scheduled departure time.

Our crew were always fit and on time but there were occasions when the aircraft were not fully serviceable. Then we would sit in the crew room and play cards. With a crew of four 'Solo' was the natural choice and this we pursued for many a long hour. After sixteen days and sixteen round trips to Berlin we returned to Brize Norton for a short break. During our time in Germany we had learned a lot. We learned that 'black marketing' was rife, to such an extent, that the street in Hanover where most of it took place had been renamed 'Schwartz Strassa' unofficially of course. Three years after the war's end many of the necessities of life were still in desperately short supply in Germany. Things like cigarettes, chocolate, and especially coffee. All through the war the

Germans had existed on 'Ersatz Coffee,' a concoction consisting mostly of ground acorn seeds and as much like coffee as 'I to Hercules.' We determined that on our return we would come armed with the wherewithal to exploit this situation.

On returning to the UK we landed first at RAF Abingdon before going on to Brize Norton. We were surprised to find no customs at all at Abingdon and as we were to be routed through Abingdon on our return to Germany and because the town was so close to the camp, which made shopping easy, we resolved to 'stock up' in this pleasant Berkshire market town immediately prior to our return.

After a ten-day break we returned to Abingdon in preparation for our onward flight to Germany the following day. We went into town with empty parachute bags and full wallets but were surprised to find that things had changed in the interim. The High Street was crawling with S.P.s (RAF Service Police) on the lookout for any airmen making unusually large purchases of anything. By carefully dodging these patrols and staggering our purchase venues we eventually managed to fill our bags with hermetically sealed tins of ground coffee. Each of us had sixty to seventy tins. Our next shock came the following morning when we found that a customs post had been established. Not to be outdone we went to see the flight's Corporal who, for a slight consideration, agreed to come to an arrangement. We handed over to him our bags of coffee and went through customs empty handed. Back in the aircraft, as soon as the engines were running a small,

THE BERLIN AIR LIFT

open backed truck came speeding out to us from the service area. As we opened the main aircraft door four large bags were hurled from the truck into the plane and we hastily took off for Germany.

On landing at Wunstorf we soon discovered that things had also changed there. The authorities were making a determined attempt to stamp out this growing black market. Everybody entering or leaving the camp would be searched. It was worse still in Berlin. The first people on the plane when we landed were the S.I.B., the Special Investigation Branch. We had all got a bag full of coffee hidden in our rooms. We had a problem. Max Chivers, our skipper, came up with the answer. With no German Government, the country was administered by an organisation known as the CCG, the Control Commission for Germany, staffed mostly by ex. Servicemen. They were housed in large houses, which were called 'Messes.' On our previous stay Max had somehow inveigled himself into one of these messes and had himself and his crew made 'honorary members.' We now called on our CCG friends for assistance. In this they excelled themselves. They sent a Wolkes Wagon Beetle, complete with German driver, into the camp to pick us up with our bags. As we drove out of the main gate we just shouted, "CCG" and were waved on.

Our route took us round the airfield and as we were passing the end of the runway a plane was taking off and rose, with a thunderous roar, above the car. We were packed like sardines and I, by the window, was the only one able to twist myself so that I could look out and up. I recognised the plane as a Hanley Page Halton, a civil version of the Halifax Bomber. "Halton!" I yelled over the din of the plane. We came to a sudden, skidding stop. The driver, who couldn't speak a word of English, looked at us questioningly. We looked back at him in the same way. Suddenly the penny dropped. 'Halten' means 'stop' in German. "No, no," I said, pointing upwards, "Halton." His expression changed to one of puzzlement and shaking his head slowly, proceeded to drive on.

He took us to the CCG mess in Hanover where we left our contraband in safe hands. They promised to contact certain people at the Volklander Camera factory in Brunswick in order to do a deal. However this had to await our next visit as there was a limit to what we could do in our thirteen-hour stand down. We had to eat, change, get into Hanover and return, and get enough sleep to be efficient flyers for the next twelve hours. Max and I would share the flying. Max, as Pilot, would do all the take-offs and landings, after which we would fly a leg each. If he flew to Berlin I would fly back and vice versa. The one who was not flying would usually go to sleep in his seat. On one occasion each thought it was the other's turn to fly and we both went to sleep. The rudder controls on the York were of the 'push-pull' type and consisted of a number of aluminium tubes that ran the length of the plane. One of these lengths of tube was alongside the Navigator's table where there was also a compass repeater. Not wanting to disturb us, the Navigator steered the plane for as long as he could by manipulating the tube. He eventually had to wake us. An argument then started between Max and me

THE BERLIN AIR LIFT

as to whose turn it was to fly. This was not a practice to be recommended because, at any time, a Soviet 'Mig' fighter could appear from nowhere and 'buzz' us. It would swoop on us in an attacking manoeuvre meant to intimidate us. We invariably ignored it and eventually they abandoned the practice.

Very often during our thirteen-hour stand-down we would stay on the camp and have a drink in the Sergeant's Mess. One evening with the bar busy and noisy, a Sergeant whom I knew not, lurched up to me and in a slightly inebriated drawl said, "I'd like you to meet the champion swimmer of the Middle East" as he pushed his 'protégé' forward. "Pleased to meet you," I replied, entering into the spirit of the thing. "I'm the champion swimmer of the Far East." They wandered off but returned about half an hour later with, "These are all the champion swimmers. We're going to have a swimming race when the bar closes, are you game?" "Sure," I replied, and thought to myself, "By then they'll all be too drunk to walk let alone swim." I was wrong. As the shutters were going up they all returned and dragged me off to the swimming pool on the camp.

The German airfields seemed better equipped than ours and an open-air, unheated swimming pool seemed a standard facility. It was a pitch-dark night and one or two of the party, which now numbered about twelve, almost fell into the pool whilst looking for it. A number of us stripped off and the four swimmers, of whom I was one, lined up for the start. On the word "go" we dived in and swam as hard as we could for the other end. Here people were groping in the water to see who had won. It was generally agreed that I was the winner but there was no prize. There was, however, a surprise. Suddenly, without warning, a diminutive Warrant Officer, a little older than most of us, gave a shriek of excitement and leapt off the high board into the pool. At first nobody took much notice. I was putting my shirt on my still wet body when I paused, thinking his re-emergence was overdue. I started to take my shirt off again. Just then there was a splash and a shriek of "Great," as he started to swim to the side. There was light and life at the aircraft servicing area at all times of the day and night and that's where we all headed for a cup of hot tea, a warm and a laugh now that we had all sobered up.

On our next visit to Hanover our CCG friends provided us with a car and a driver who took us 50 miles along the autobahn to Brunswick. This was our first experience of travelling on a motorway. The first motorways in the UK did not appear until ten years later. We met our appointees at the Volklander Camera Factory, armed with our bags of coffee and ready to do a deal. The Germans however were not fully prepared. They examined our offerings and promised to come over to Hanover with a selection of cameras. They were as good as their word and at our next visit they arrived at the CCG mess with 'the goods.' They looked quite a formidable group. One of them wore 'Jack Boots.' They proved to be less menacing however and we soon made a deal that suited us both. The Germans, as a nation, seemed to be very militaristic. During the war we were told that, when an allied airman was captured, he would be interrogated

THE BERLIN AIR LIFT

by all manner of means even with threats of being shot. If they obtained no information from their prisoner his papers would be stamped 'Guten Soldat' (Good Soldier) and he would be sent to a prison camp. Most of the Germans that we mixed with must have been aware that we were the same people who had been bombing them three years before. Yet they treated us with respect and even admiration.

When we were off duty in the evenings we would often 'exercise our right, as honorary members,' to visit the mess in Hanover where the main pastime was partying. A number of interesting characters would appear. On one occasion I got talking to a man who could have been an airman in civilian clothes. He was using all the current RAF slang. He gave me a sudden surprise when he referred to Hitler as the 'Fuhrer.' "Who is he?" I asked somebody later. "He's our interpreter," was the reply, "He used to be an interrogator. He would interrogate prisoners when they were first captured."

Our CCG friends would do their best to dissuade us from 'going on the town.' They would remind us that V.D. was rife. One night during a visit from one of the Wireless Operators from our unit back at Brize Norton, he and I decided to sample the nightlife. My companion's name was Evans but we always called him 'Tish.' There were two Evans's on the unit and to identify them we called them 'Tish and Tosh.' Tish and I found a nightclub and sat ourselves down at a table where a girl was sitting on her own. We soon found that the girl could not speak a word of English and neither of us spoke any German. We found an ingenious solution to the problem. Tish had been in Italy during the war and had picked up a spattering of Italian. The German waiter had also been in Italy and the two were able to have a rudimentary conversation in Italian. When I wanted to say anything to the girl I would say it in English to Tish, he would say it in Italian to the waiter, and the waiter would say it in German to the girl. It was hard to say what was lost or gained in the translation but ultimately the girl acquiesced to our suggestion that she return to the mess with us.

On our return to the mess our CCG friends, who had warned us against the German girls, started to show a lively interest in her. They had the advantage of speaking a little German but the girl remained loyal to me and at a late hour we found a secluded spot in the grounds. Things were just becoming interesting between us when there was a shout from the doorway of the house. "Dead Head - Flying!" It was Max telling us that it was time for us to return to camp for our next spell of flying. Of course duty came first and as we left I saw our CCG friends crowding round the girl and vying with each other for her attentions. I never saw her again but often wondered how things had turned out after we left.

By the time we had been in Germany for a total of some six weeks, and had made about fifty round trips to Gatow, in Berlin, the organisation had become firmly established. More and more civil aircraft were taking part and it was felt that our solitary York with its crew would be better employed at home helping to develop the many projects that we had been working on. We went into Hanover for the last time

THE BERLIN AIR LIFT

to say good-bye to our friends. The Scottish chairman of the mess and leader of the gang offered to buy our German currency from us. The mark at that time was worthless in the UK, and so we eagerly accepted his offer. He gave us his cheque, drawn on a British bank, for a significant sum in sterling. When we tried to cash his cheque in England it was refused. There was no resentment however as we were agreed that it was a fair price to pay for all the help that they had given us.

Max was nothing if not resourceful. We found that he had somehow arranged for us to be routed home through RAF Dishforth, in Yorkshire, where there was no customs. When we arrived at Dishforth we found that there was customs of a sort. It consisted of a young junior RAF Officer with no training who was in awe of the older and more senior Officers that he had to deal with. As a result we all walked past him, some with camera case straps trailing out of our pockets, and all of us shouting, "Nothing to declare." I myself brought back a good camera which I later sold to the civilian representative of the Bristol Aircraft Company who was based on the camp at Brize Norton. He paid me the princely sum of £29 for it and at that time £29 was indeed a princely sum.

11
RELOCATION

Shortly after our return to Brize Norton we acquired two new types of Transport Planes the Vickers Valletta and the Hanley Page Hastings. They were both wide-bodied aircraft of a new design. The first to arrive was the Valletta which was a twin engined, medium range, transport. It did not normally carry a Flight Engineer but to help their confidence during the familiarisation process the Pilots preferred to have one on board. As a result I flew a fair number of hours in the Valletta, including a trip to Malta. Because of its limited range we had to make a refuelling stop at Istres, a French Air Force base near Marseille. Because I was not expecting to require any oil at this stop, my roommate, Mall, who could speak a bit of French, had taught me to say, "Pas d' oile." When I dipped the oil tanks I found that they did need topping up. Imagine my relief when, at that moment, a French speaking RAF Liaison Officer arrived on the scene.

A couple of weeks later, the Hastings arrived. This was a four engined, long-range transport, which was better than anything that we had seen before. The Flight Engineer had his own desk and chair and a complete set of duplicate controls and instruments. The plane even had a little rest room with a bed. W/Cdr. Scragg, the CO, showed a lively interest in the plane quickly getting to know its characteristics and capabilities and insisting on all his Pilots doing the same. At the end of November we took the plane to Sleswigland, in Northern Germany. We stopped the night and returned to base the next day. The weather seemed a lot colder in Sleswigland than in England and after a night out in town, I was waiting for the transport back to the airfield, rubbing my hands and stamping my feet for warmth. Nearby a German civilian was doing the same. "Iss colt," he said to me. "Ya," I replied, "Iss verr colt." 'This German language is easy,' I said to myself. 'All you have to do is to speak English with a funny accent.'

One of the projects that we were developing at this time was an automatic Pilot for gliders and an instrument for indicating the position of the tug aircraft when flying in cloud which we dubbed 'Angle of Dangle.' We were doing a lot of glider towing and on one occasion, I was flying in a Halifax with a Canadian Pilot who was not very experienced at glider towing. We were doing a cross-country flight in cloud. The Pilot started to turn onto his final leg for home. I thought the turn was a bit tight for the glider and when I noticed the air speed start to build up I said to the Pilot, "I think we may have lost the glider, shall I check?" "Yes please," he said, nervously. I went to the rear end of the fuselage, to where the towrope release mechanism was, and looked out through the aperture. Sure enough there was the rope snaking loosely in mid air. "I'm afraid I was right," I said on my return, "We'd better notify base."

Back at base we learned that the glider had been forced to cast off, as the turn was too tight. When they broke cloud they were over the Bristol Channel and the Pilot, my good friend Army Sergeant Dinger Bell, had successfully landed the glider on a football field in Cardiff. For this he was later awarded the MBE. Had he been in the RAF he would have received the DFM (Distinguished Flying Medal).

In the service, people were only called by their first names if nobody could think of a suitable nickname. Bells were always called Dinger. Dinger was a man after my own heart. He was always laid back and completely unflappable and with a lively sense of humour. One day, whilst suffering from a nasty stomach upset, I was in his room, sprawled out on his bed whilst he was trying to explain to me how our football pool syndicate might have won a dividend had he not forgotten to post the coupon. At the time I used caster oil as a hair-oil and also as a panacea for all stomach problems. "I'll have to drink my hair oil," I groaned. "Oh you don't have to resort to that," he said, "It's not that serious." I had to laugh though as I downed the oil, feeling like death.

As Dinger was the glider Pilot for the glider snatching operation and Mall, my roommate, was a Winch Operator, I often involved myself in the glider snatching operation which was a star attraction at Air Shows. Having operated the winch on one or two snatches I decided to sample the glider. The rate of acceleration was out of this world. 0 – 120 mph in 5 seconds. About twice as fast as a formula one racing car.

In March, I was sent on a two weeks Hastings course to the Hanley Page Factory at Radlet, in Hertfordshire. One other Flight Engineer and I were the only RAF people on the course. The remainder were all civilians employed at RAF Maintenance Units. One day, at dinner in the canteen, one of the civilian lads produced a home made, pocket-sized card folded in two. On the outside was written in big letters, 'WOMENS' RATION CARD,' and underneath, 'To be taken at night.' When the folded card was opened it revealed a very life like and life size picture of a man's genitals. In addition the large penis was arranged so that, on the opening of the card, the penis would rise into an erect position. As the owner went up for his meal he nonchalantly handed the card to the girl serving behind the counter with, "Have you seen this?" The girl opened it then let out a shriek and dropped it like a hot brick. She quickly retrieved it and took it into the kitchen at the back. We always knew where it was from the screams that periodically emanated from the kitchen.

I finished the manufacturer's course with a final mark of 'B', 80%. Shortly after my return we had a visit from the Transport Command Examining Unit for a categorisation on the Hastings. In this I did even better. I managed a 'B+' Category, which represented 85% as my lowest mark on any

RELOCATION

one subject. This was a thorough assessment since a failure in one subject could fail you altogether.

In the spring of 1949 we received a visit from two separate photographic units. One was a full film crew who spent two or three weeks with us. We never found out who the film was for but we quite enjoyed taking the camera crew up in the Hastings for the air-to-air shots. The director and his entourage used the Officer's Mess while the lowly 'Continuity Girl' used the Sergeant's Mess. She was quite attractive and we felt sure that none of the Officers had seen her before these arrangements were made otherwise she would have been in the Officer's Mess.

The other unit was a single, still photographer from Air Ministry. He had come to take photographs for a recruiting pamphlet. He wanted the latest aircraft in service which were the Hastings and the Valletta. For the Hastings he wanted the Flight Engineer to be an NCO rather than an Officer. The only other unit with these aircraft was the Examining Unit and their crews were all Officers and so he came to Brize Norton. Jock Jack and I were the only NCO Flight Engineers and Jock Jack was away somewhere flying on the day that the photographer arrived. That is how I was 'specially selected' for this prestigious task. Some weeks after this, one of my friends said to me, "I was walking past the Air Ministry this afternoon when I had a terrible shock. There in the window was a larger-than-life size picture of you. It gave me quite a fright."

Having my own home in England resulted in the loosening of my contacts with my wartime adopted family. However, I was not entirely out of touch and when I received an invitation to Paddy's wedding I was determined to be there. He was now stationed at RAF Horsham-Saint-Faith, near Norwich. The wedding was scheduled for early on a Saturday afternoon and to get there on time, leaving after work on Friday, would have involved either a night journey or an overnight stop in Norwich. Lady luck came to my aid. One of our Dakotas was flying to Horsham-Saint-Faith on that Saturday morning. I had no difficulty in getting a lift and they were all surprised and delighted when I turned up at the church for a mini re-union with Paddy, his bride, Doreen, his mother and his brother Des, now a civilian.

In May, there was none on the unit that had any regrets when W/Cdr. Scragg left and was replaced by W/Cdr. Griffiths. It seemed hardly possible for two Commanding Officers to be so different. W/Cdr. Scragg was a super efficient perfectionist and a strict disciplinarian. At sometime in the 1960s I happened to pick up a copy of the magazine 'Flight' in a waiting room somewhere and saw a reference to the retirement of Air vice Marshal Scragg. W/Cdr. Griffiths on the other hand was a soft-spoken, rather gentle, very humane Officer, who always led from the front. One very chilly morning, the two of us were walking out to our aircraft when he noticed my hands turning a shade of blue. "Put your hands in your pockets if they're cold, Gould" he said. Something that was strictly forbidden when in uniform.

RELOCATION

When he arrived on the unit, he brought with him, a little Auster, single engined two-seater aeroplane that belonged to him. There was also a RAF Auster on the station. He wanted to take his plane back to the factory at Syston, near Leicester, to have a modification carried out so he asked Dinger Bell, who was also a small-plane Pilot, to follow him and bring him back. Dinger, who always seemed to be catching up on time, grabbed his flying helmet and maps, and jumped into the RAF Auster and took off. When he was airborne he realised that he had only got one of the two maps needed to cover the area between our base and the factory. He soon found himself lost when he ran out of map but, nothing daunted, he looked over the side and spotted a farmer ploughing an unused wartime airfield, that was being returned to nature. The runway was still intact and so he landed on this, taxied up to the farmer, who was on his tractor, and shouted across, "Which way to Leicester?" "It be that way," was the answer as the farmer pointed in the general direction. "Thanks," said Dinger, took off again, and headed in the direction indicated. He managed to find the factory and brought the CO back. Whether the CO was ever aware of this fiasco or not, Dinger did not say, but it never became an issue.

It was about this time that I had a rather puzzling experience. I saw an Army Lieutenant whom I was sure I knew. I thought I recognised him as being an old school boy. I went up to him and asked, "Aren't you 'McIver the Diver?" At the school swimming sports he always won the diving. Rather reluctantly he agreed that he was but showed no excitement at the idea of meeting a school old boy under such unusual circumstances.

"Perhaps that's the way they do it in the Army," I thought. In the RAF the aircrew Officers and NCOs regarded each other almost as mates. However a few days later we were taking a party of soldiers, in the Hastings, on an air experience flight. He was the Officer in charge of the party who were already seated in the aircraft when we started to board. As I walked passed them he called out, "Hello Peter." "Ah," I thought, "Now he's trying to impress his men by showing them that he's on first name terms with the crew."

Although the new aircraft were very popular with the crews, we still had to fly the older ones, like the Halifax. These Halifaxs were an adaptation of the bomber. They retained the bomb bay but dispensed with the gun turrets and other equipment to provide a large open space in the rear fuselage. This was to house the parachutists, mainly for training purposes. The parachutists would leave the aircraft through a large hatch in the floor.

The bomb compartment was used to carry a Field Gun and Jeep which were dropped by parachute. It was the responsibility of the Navigator to release these as there were no Bomb Aimers in Transport Command. Eventually the development reached the stage where the gun and jeep were housed in a single container known as a 'Pannier.' This was dropped on three or four parachutes and to cushion the impact on landing, the whole of the bottom of the pannier was covered with a large inflated air bag that was allowed to burst on impact.

RELOCATION

On one occasion we were about to do a test drop. As we approached the airfield at about 500 ft. the Navigator was setting his bomb release switches in readiness for the drop, when he inadvertently pressed the wrong switch and released the pannier. The pannier successfully parachuted to earth but landed in the back garden of a country cottage occupied by an elderly couple. They got the fright of their lives when an enormous Field Gun and Jeep arrived out of the sky with a loud bang.

There was always a sister unit from the Army on the base with us. Our unit was the Transport Command Development Unit, TCDU for short. Not to be outdone, the Army unit had one letter more. They were the A.A.T.D.C., which stood for Army Airborne Transport Development Corp. At the end of June, both units moved en-mass from Brize Norton to RAF Abingdon, then in Berkshire. The reason for the move was that Brize Norton had been leased to the US Air Force. This was the start of the 'fifty years war.' The 'Cold War' and the Americans were coming back to Europe. In Abingdon another Army unit, the Parachute Training School, joined us and very soon all the paraphernalia associated with parachuting, such as crane-like towers with power lifts etc., were being installed. On the day of the move Mall and I travelled in our own vehicles, he on his motorcycle and I in my car. We arrived early at Abingdon to secure the best accommodation. We found that the Sergeant's Mess was a sprawling, single storey building, with numerous little rooms, known as 'bunks,' which accommodated all the senior NCOs. We immediately laid claim to the one on the extreme end of the wing because it had an emergency door adjacent outside which was ample parking space for our vehicles. I had in mind another advantage. Mall was married and went home every weekend, leaving me alone in the room with its convenient location for introducing 'uninvited guests.'

Not long before we moved to Abingdon, a number of us made one of our occasional visits to Cheltenham. Although it was our favourite venue for a Saturday night out, the lack of public transport to Cheltenham made it difficult to get to and so whenever the opportunity presented itself we would take it. The weekly dance in the town hall had a bar insitu and rumour had it that females in Cheltenham outnumbered males by five to one. On this occasion I met a girl at the dance. She was fairly attractive and we got on well together. Her name was Cynthia and she told me that she was in the W.R.N.S. (Women's Royal Naval Service), that she lived in Cheltenham and that she was home on leave. I told her that we were moving to Abingdon yet we agreed to keep in touch though another meeting seemed to have its problems. I underestimated her because within a couple of weeks she had got herself transferred to the Royal Naval Air Station at Culham, some 5 miles from RAF Abingdon on the other side of the town. We soon drifted into a relationship, more casual than intense.

On the last few occasions that I had been home on leave I found that my sister, Rosalie, was bringing home a different boyfriend each time. I thought to myself, "Well if she can do it, why can't I?" So for my next leave Cynthia and I had

RELOCATION

a week together which we spent half at my parent's home and half at hers. This prompted my mother to ask me if my intentions were serious. I avoided a direct answer though I did wonder why she never asked Rosalie the same question. At the time I would have a series of girlfriends none of whom I had any intention of marrying nor did I give them any reason to think otherwise. On one occasion I made it plain to a girl whom I had just met that my intentions did not extend to marriage. I soon found out that this merely acted as a challenge, after which I desisted from being so direct.

After a few weeks I began to get a little concerned that Cynthia was taking our relationship too seriously and I tried to cool it a bit. When an opportunity arose for a night out in Cheltenham I told her that I was on duty and went out. It proved to be an enjoyable but uneventful evening. Early the next morning I was rudely awakened by the unit Warrant Officer, the Army Regimental Sergeant Major and one or two others who resented their inability to exercise their authority over young 'whipper snappers' like me who were of equal rank to them. Seizing the opportunity they burst into my room with shouts of, "Well where is she?" They were a little taken aback when they saw me alone and started looking under the bed. "What are you looking for?" I asked. "Your WRN girlfriend," they said, "She's missing." "I haven't seen her for a couple of days," I said. "Then she's probably deserted," they concluded. I eventually discovered that she had somehow arrived on the RAF camp in a naval transport and took the opportunity to try and locate me. It must have been quite a blow for her to realise that I was not on duty, and that I had gone out socialising. She had indeed deserted which, strangely enough, was not an offence in the WRNS. I never saw her again.

When we first moved to Abingdon and I walked into the Sergeant's Mess lounge I quickly spotted a familiar face. It was a Sergeant named Cooke. He was one of the boys in the group that had come over with me from India. I got a cool reception when I spoke to him however, and it was not long before I found out why. He had always been one of those multi-talented achievers. Head boy in school, a boy Sergeant at Halton, boxing champion, winner of the dance competition at Halton. These were just some of his achievements. I always felt that he looked on me as an inferior being and we were never on friendly terms. Then suddenly here I was, two ranks above him in seniority and what seemed to rankle him even more, that I was still single. He had got married young, to a WAAF whom he met at Halton, and now, seven years later, the guilt had worn off the gingerbread and he envied my social and sexual freedom. He was not alone in this. Many of my comrades were married and most seemed to envy my single state. One day a Sergeant, a little older than myself, said to me in a fatherly way, "You know at your age you shouldn't be sleeping alone." "I know," I replied, dismissively, "I try not to."

Our new location by the river Thames offered more scope for active dinghy drill and in my position as Survival and Rescue Officer, I explored the river for a suitable venue. This I found in a pretty little village called Sutton Courtney, where a small loop off the main river had two weirs between which was formed a large pool. On our first visit, and each succeeding one, as soon as we were changed and the dinghy inflated, I completely lost control of the class. Most of them were Officers and older than me, yet they all behaved like children. Laughing and shouting they all jumped into the water and started a game of attackers and defenders with the dinghy. As I was not able to control them I joined in. On one exercise I thought it would be a good idea to see if it was practical to pluck a man out of the dinghy with a helicopter. The Army had a small helicopter which was flown by an Army Officer. This was before the days of winches and Winch Operators in large rescue helicopters. All we had was a rope ladder, which was trailed out of the open door. The senior RAF Officer was a Squadron Leader. He was a humourless individual but with lots of enthusiasm. He agreed to be the guinea pig, and we cast him adrift in the dinghy. As soon as he had got a firm hold on the third or fourth rung of the ladder, the helicopter Pilot, by agreement with the rest of us, lifted the Squadron Leader out of the dinghy, took him clear, and hovered over the middle of the river until he could hold on no longer. He fell into the river, fully clothed, accompanied by loud applause from the bank.

September 15th was always known as 'Battle of Britain Day' and on the nearest Saturday, most RAF stations were open to the public for static displays and fly-pasts. The year before we had been in Germany, on the Berlin Air Lift, and had not been able to take part. This year, 1949, we were able to give a good performance. As usual 'the glider snatch' was the main attraction at Abingdon. As the Hastings was such a new aircraft and only two were in service, it was decided to show it all round the country. We flew from one station to the next, flying low across each airfield on three engines with one engine feathered. Our itinerary included Gatwick which at that time was still a RAF base.

A lot of RAF bases were in remote areas but Abingdon was an exception. It was within easy walking distance of the town which had enough amenities to offer a good social life. It became a ritual on a Saturday night to assemble in the 'Red Lion' for drinks until they closed at ten o'clock. We would then make our way to the dance at the Church Hall or the Assembly Rooms. One uneventful Saturday night a small group of us felt quite disappointed that nothing exciting had happened. Somebody suggested that London never slept and on impulse, we piled into my car and set off for the west end. By the time we got there, some two hours later, we had all sobered up and we wondered what we were doing there. The west end of London, in the early hours of the morning, was too expensive a place for poorly paid airmen. So we turned round and drove all the way back to camp again.

On another occasion the evening proved quite different. As we entered the dance hall, I saw a stunningly attractive girl across the other side of the room. It reminded me of the song, 'Some enchanted evening, you may see a stranger, across a crowded room.' I asked her for a dance and discovered that her name was Kathleen. I asked if I could take her home but she turned me down, saying that her boyfriend was coming to pick her up when the dance finished. Her boyfriend proved to be the landlord of the 'Red Lion,' a young man whose wealthy parents had bought the pub for him to manage. I knew him of course and decided to take him on in competition for Kath's attentions. The opportunity came a couple of weeks later when I bumped into her at the entrance to the dance hall. I tried to persuade her to come into the dance but she protested that she was not suitably dressed and intended getting a taxi home. I offered her a lift in my car which she accepted. To my surprise I found that she lived in the pretty little village of Sutton Courtenay where we did our dinghy drill. We spent a long time sitting in the car outside her house talking and getting to know each other. Our association soon became an affair, when she was often referred to as 'Gould's Woman.'

In October we took the Hastings on an overseas trip. The pretext was altitude take-offs and the destination was Nairobi, in Kenya, 4000ft. above sea level. We had two crews on board and a few passengers, one of whom was my roommate Mall. As usual our first night stop was Malta and when it was discovered that Jock Jack, the other Flight Engineer, had caught a cold, he was immediately grounded and we went on without him. He spent the next ten days sunning himself in Malta and ridding himself of his cold so that he could be picked up on our return to the UK.

Our next stop was Fayed, in the Suez Canal Zone. The British had pulled out of Egypt but retained a military presence along the canal. The following day, we landed at Khartoum in the 'Sunny Sudan.' This is where the Blue Nile and the White Nile meet. Looking at them though, we wondered why they were called 'Blue' and 'White' as they were both a dirty brown and as rumour had it, if you fell in, you would need to be filled with 'jabs.' It was nine o'clock at night when we settled into our rooms and the walls of the building were still warm. This gave us an indication of what to expect in the morning. The plan was to have a day off in Khartoum and in the morning we got a lift into town in a car belonging to a British civilian. There was so little traffic about that when he got to his destination he parked the car in the middle of the road. In the afternoon we went swimming in an unheated swimming pool where the water was luke warm from the sun. The following day we arrived at our destination, RAF Eastleigh, Nairobi.

We did one take off on each of the following two days and spent the rest of the time on safari in a nearby game reserve and also shopping in Nairobi. Unintentionally I got myself a little wooden carving of a native warrior. Sitting on the side of the road was a Kikuyu tribesman whittling away at a small piece of black African hard wood. As we came past he offered to sell us one that he had already made. We rejected him but he kept following us and periodically lowering his price. I thought I knew a way to get rid of him. I offered him a ridiculously low figure which, to my surprise, he accepted. I then had no option but to buy. When I examined it more closely I was quite impressed and kept it with pride. In later years, my four very young children succeeded in destroying it.

RELOCATION

Mall had some friends in Nairobi and one night we went to dinner at their bungalow. It was only a light meal and they asked us which we would prefer, eggs or kippers. Eggs were a rare delicacy in the UK in those days and unthinkingly we said, "Kippers." Their faces fell. Then we realised that kippers, which were commonplace to us at home, were a treat in Kenya. "No, no - eggs," we said, "We prefer eggs." Their faces lit up again as they served our preferences.

Most of the RAF stations overseas, especially the ones near the country's capitals, like Palam at Delhi and now Eastleigh for Nairobi, had small Terminal Buildings in preparation for their ultimate role as international airports. Whilst in the terminal building at Eastleigh we bumped into a couple of wartime RAF comrades. They were now civilians, employed on the 'Ground Nuts Scheme,' and were heading back to the UK on home leave. The Ground Nuts Scheme was a UK government sponsored scheme. It involved clearing large tracts of land in Tanganyika, later Tanzania, in order to grow peanuts. These would be crushed to produce oil for cooking and for the manufacture of certain foods, such as margarine. In hindsight it was an ill-considered idea based on the false assumption that the British Empire was going to last a thousand years. A few years later the whole thing was abandoned as a costly failure. We also got talking to a RAF aircrew NCO who had been on the particular unit at Abingdon which our unit had displaced. He knew my new girlfriend Kath which was not surprising as she stood out among the Abingdon girls.

Our return to the UK took an uneventful four days picking up Jock Jack at Malta, his cold now being better. In the evening we made the usual visit to 'The Gut' in Valletta. We stopped at a bar, which bore a notice, 'Officers and Gentlemen Only.' Realising that this was only a ploy to raise the image of the premises we all went in. There was the usual bevy of hostesses plying for drinks and one of them attached herself to us standing alongside Jonah, our Wireless Operator. Although he was chatting her up he made no attempt to buy her a drink. After a while she turned to him and said, angrily, "You are naughty boy, you never buy me drink. All you want to do is stroke my bloody arse."

The following month we did a short trip in the Hastings to Egypt This time W/Cdr. Griffiths, our new CO, was the Captain and the experience was in sharp contrast to the trips with his predecessor. The purpose of the trip was to try out rear facing seats and to test certain Anti-Airsickness Drugs. The passengers were almost all volunteers from the Army and also included a young RAF Medical Officer. Again we had two crews and this time Jock Jack stayed with us all the way. It was my turn to fly the first leg of the return journey and whilst waiting for everybody to board the aircraft, the MO gave me a pill to swallow. I thought nothing of it at the time but halfway through the flight to Malta, I had difficulty in handling the power settings and also became very irritable, snapping back rudely at the CO when he enquired about my welfare. Eventually I was persuaded to let Jock Jack take over while I lay on the rest bed. I immediately went into a deep sleep and awoke just before we landed in Malta. Whatever

RELOCATION

I had done to the power settings, Jock had been forced to feather one of the engines and we did a three engined landing. As we walked away from the plane, I was trailing a few paces behind the CO and Jonah, the Wireless Operator, and overheard their conversation. "I wonder what the trouble was with Gould," the CO said. "I reckon it was the pill the Doc gave him," replied Jonah. "What?" exclaimed the CO "He gave him one of those pills? I know what they are, they're Barbiturates. The man's a menace, he's going back home on the next plane." The next plane was not ours, because though we had landed on three engines, we could not take off on three.

We now had to address ourselves to the task of replacing the faulty engine. One of our passengers was a Sergeant Fitter and he, Jock and I formed the team for the job. We were rather hoping that we could get hold of a complete 'Power Plant.' This would have meant merely taking off the propeller, with the help of a crane of course, disconnecting all the unions at the bulkhead, releasing the engine bearer bolts and removing the whole assembly. The replacement power plant would reverse the procedure. Unfortunately there was no power plant on the base and to get one flown out from the UK would take a fortnight. There was an engine in the stores but this was very basic and lacked all the essential components such as an oil pump, alternator, hydraulic pump etc. With Christmas only twelve days away, we resolved on this option and the three of us set about the mammoth task of transferring all the components from one engine to the other. We worked twenty hours a day, in the open and under arc lights, though the Maltese climate was kind to us. During all this time the only person from the plane who came near us was the CO He would bring us hot drinks in a vacuum flask, sometimes after midnight. He said, "I can't be much help to you technically but at least I can help to keep you going." Here was a leader we would have followed anywhere. We finished the job in five days and got back to Abingdon five days before Christmas.

Christmas on the camp promised to be more fun than going home and this is what I chose. It included an elaborate dance in the Sergeant's Mess to which most of the local girls were invited. I intentionally omitted to send Kath an invitation as I did not yet feel committed. I wanted to see what developed. However she was there, invited by one of her many admirers, and we spent the evening together.

In the New Year having guests in the mess on a Saturday night became a frequent occurrence. One Saturday night in February, I took Kath to the mess with some of our friends. We all got into a party mood and Kath had a bit too much to drink. Needing to get her sober before I could take her home, we went to my room with the intention of drinking black coffee. After brewing the coffee with a makeshift kettle and stove Mall and I had devised out of an upturned iron and a billycan, Kath and I sat on my bed sipping the warm brew. Since Mall had gone home for the weekend we found that we were alone and soon we inevitably got into the bed. Though we had little inkling at the time, this was the night when our son Christopher was conceived.

12
REFLECTIONS

With only three months to go to my discharge date my mind turned to reflections on the past and possible prospects for the future. Very soon I had a big decision to make, whether to terminate my service or to extend it for a further indeterminate period. I began to reflect on the small incidents that could have such devastating consequences. In particular I thought about our unauthorised occupation of a room in the Sergeant's Mess when we first arrived on the Pathfinder Squadron at Coningsby and the ultimate consequences that cost me a commission. I was reminded of a line from Shakespeare's Julius Caesar, "There is a tide in the affairs of men, which, taken at flood, leads on to fortune. Omitted, all the voyage of their days is bound in shallows and in miseries." "That's me," I thought, "as far as my career is concerned, 'bound in shallows and in miseries'." If I had not made that mistake I would almost certainly have been awarded a commission and my career would have taken off. This was confirmed in the years that followed when I read about ex Halton apprentices like W/Cdr. Scragg, who rose to be an Air vice Marshal and a lad from the same entry as me at Halton who, as a Group Captain, became the Commanding Officer at Halton.

I consoled myself with the thought, "It wasn't meant to be," and this philosophy has stood me in good stead all my life. I also reflected on another line from Shakespeare's Hamlet, "There's a divinity that shapes our ends, rough-hew them how we will." "Whatever lies ahead for me," I thought, "is meant to be." Because I failed to get a commission perhaps I was not meant to make the RAF a career and my thoughts turned to the prospects of life as a civilian. I had never experienced civilian life in Britain and my curiosity tugged me in that direction.

I thought also about the two incidents that together had ensured my stay of nine months in India. The collusion between Rene's husband and my CO ensuring my early despatch, coupled with the contraction of VD by the Flight Engineer in the first crew, and my replacement of him. Without either of these incidents, I would have been sent to No. 1 Ferry Unit, at RAF Pershore, where I would have spent my days travelling the world. I would almost certainly not have gone to Abingdon where I met Kath, and all the implications that then had for my descendants.

I also reflected on the ten years that I had spent in the RAF and my thoughts went back to that day in the school library

REFLECTIONS

in 1939, and Mr. Serdival's words, "And they'll be the best twelve years of your life." Would they prove to be the best years? By and large they had certainly been good times especially the latter years. Full of great experiences, variety and excitement. These were the heady days of irresponsible youth that could never be recaptured. Perhaps it was time to change direction. To try a new experience. The civilian experience.

Having decided to go down that road I began to explore the choice of occupations. Number one was the airlines and I wrote to all the English speaking ones at home and abroad. I was turned down by all which did not surprise me as there was still a glut of wartime-trained flyers everywhere.

About this time I attended two big RAF functions in London. One was a Bomber Command Reunion at the Albert Hall. My guests, who accompanied me, were my cousin Pam who was living in London and studying at London University, and also her new boyfriend, John, who had been in the Navy, and was a mature student at the university, where they had met. The hall contained some ten thousand ex Bomber Command personnel and though I mixed freely among them I did not meet a soul I knew.

The other function, which took place before the Reunion, was the 'Pathfinder Ball' held at the Dorchester Hotel in Park Lane. I took my cousin Pam with me to this, mainly because it was a paired function and it was nice to have a companion with whom I felt at ease. The 'Guests of Honour' were the stars of the film, 'The Way to the Stars,' a story of wartime RAF exploits. They were John Mills, Trevor Howard and Rosamond Johns. I got talking to their minder who had been hovering around them. I told him that I intended leaving the RAF soon. He gave me his visiting card and said, "Come and see me when you do. I'll fix you up with a job." I took him at his word and a couple of weeks before I left I called at the address on the card which was titled 'The Rank Organisation' and asked for him. "He doesn't work here any more," the girl told me, "He's been fired."

As one avenue of exploration closed I turned to another. For the last three years I had kept in contact with my friend, Peter Payne. He was the lad who had shared with me the epic 'Tonga' ride from Delhi station to Palam in 1946. His father owned a catering employment agency in the West End of London. I arranged to meet him in 'The Swiss Cottage,' a well-known London landmark and near to where he lived. As I entered I saw him standing at the bar talking to a middle-aged gentleman. Peter introduced him to me as the Sales Manager of 'Claude-General Neon Signs,' a subsidiary of G.E.C. (General Electric Co.). After we had been chatting for an hour the gentleman turned to Peter and said about me, "You know he'd make a bloody good rep." I thought to myself, "Ah, that's something I hadn't thought of, especially a technical representative. For the last seven years I had been talking technically rather than working with my hands. It may be something that I could be good at." I kept it in mind for future possibilities.

REFLECTIONS

Meanwhile, back at Abingdon my relationship with Kath was developing steadily. Neither of us knew what would become of it once I had left. I half expected it to fade out. I wasn't quite sure how Kath felt but she kept singing me a song that was popular at the time. "You're breaking my heart 'cos you're leaving." An English version of the Italian love song 'Mattinata'.

When the day came we said goodbye without tears. I went to the demob centre near Blackpool and got another civilian suit, then went home on two weeks demob leave. I found that my brother, David, who was also in the RAF, was on leave at the same time. On the spur of the moment we decided to have a low budget holiday in Paris for a week. There were no 'Package Holidays' in those days and our financial resources were severely strained. We both enjoyed the week but strangely, I found myself missing Kath. The only postcard that I sent back to England I sent to her. It displayed a close-up picture of one of the gargoyles on Notre Dame Cathedral. On the back I told her I was sending her a picture of myself in Paris. On our return we crossed the channel from Dieppe to New Haven where the customs were not so much interested in contraband as currency. There was strict currency control at the time and I was asked, "How much money have you got?" "Six pence" I replied. He turned to my brother and said, "And I suppose you're the same?" "Certainly not," replied David, "I've got one and six."

Shortly after we got back to the family home in Birmingham, I hurriedly returned to Abingdon to see Kath. I was greeted with the startling news that she was pregnant. "That's decided it," I said, "We'll get married, OK?" Kath readily agreed and not yet being eighteen at the time, we required her father's consent. Her parents had always had a stormy relationship and she had been reluctant to take me home.

Eventually Kath and I took our courage in both hands and I was introduced to her parents. Her Mother, who I was meeting for the first time, proved to be a fun loving woman in her fifties, already greying, with a loud laugh, especially when unaccompanied by her more serious husband. She also had a fine disregard for, what most people consider, the important things in life, like money and property. Strangely though, in a sense I was meeting her father for the second time. Some time previously I had learned that he worked as a civilian employee in the Officer's Mess and one morning as 'Guard Commander' I had taken the opportunity to identify him as he checked into work. I found him to be a small man, about 5ft. 6in., thin and rather elderly looking for his age. I seemed to meet their approval, as he agreed to sign the relevant documentation and after I had taken Kath home to meet my parents, we were ready to arrange a wedding cermony.

I was still unemployed and unable to support a wife, so with renewed urgency, I managed to obtain a job as a Sales Representative with Remington Rand, selling typewriters to industry. The last hurdle cleared, we were married in Birmingham, and spent a short honeymoon in Aberystwyth.

I had certainly changed direction. It was now 1950 and in a single year I had gone from a young, irresponsible bachelor airman, to a responsible, married, civilian parent, seeking to become a house owner. It was quite an experience, and we now both looked forward to the adventures this new life would bring.

APPENDIX

THE IMMORTAL TEN THOUSAND

Time was in the early nineteen forties
When half the world was once again at war,
Brave young men flew out on nightly sorties
To hostile lands beyond their native shore.

These were the men the new historian slanders
Who gave their lives to save the land we love,
Not down in the killing fields of Flanders
But in the black forbidding skies above.

Ten thousand was at most their front line strength.
Like 'The Immortal Ten Thousand' of yore,
New men replaced the fallen 'till at length
A hundred thousand fell throughout the war.

As they droned their way through the starry night,
Searchlights, the sparkle of exploding shells
And the Night Fighter, that most dreaded sight,
Would oft-times alternate with quiet spells.

Then in a thrice the darkness was aflame,
A patch of glittering silver on the ground.
A badge of death and 'Target' was its name,
With skill and stealth in darkness it was found.

Soon that patch with yellow flames erupted,
As every plane let go its lethal load.
That was how each crew had been instructed,
And nothing then their purpose would erode.

And those below, there's none for them would weep,
Or ever think about those ghastly scenes.
For those were days when human life was cheap,
The end would always justify the means.

Then as they turned and set a course for base,
They saw around them little floating fires.
Deep in their hearts they knew in every case,
That what they saw were comrades' funeral pyres.

As ever in this war-torn world of strife,
The all too familiar tragic story.
They received in payment for a short life,
Their reward, eternal youth and glory.

Peter Gould

ISBN 141205523-7